Cambridge Elements ≡

Elements in Political Economy
edited by
David Stasavage
New York University

REPRESENTATION AND TAXATION IN THE AMERICAN SOUTH 1820–1910

Jeffrey L. Jensen
New York University–Abu Dhabi

Giuliana Pardelli
New York University–Abu Dhabi

Jeffrey F. Timmons
New York University–Abu Dhabi

CAMBRIDGE
UNIVERSITY PRESS

Shaftesbury Road, Cambridge CB2 8EA, United Kingdom

One Liberty Plaza, 20th Floor, New York, NY 10006, USA

477 Williamstown Road, Port Melbourne, VIC 3207, Australia

314–321, 3rd Floor, Plot 3, Splendor Forum, Jasola District Centre,
New Delhi – 110025, India

103 Penang Road, #05–06/07, Visioncrest Commercial, Singapore 238467

Cambridge University Press is part of Cambridge University Press & Assessment,
a department of the University of Cambridge.

We share the University's mission to contribute to society through the pursuit of
education, learning and research at the highest international levels of excellence.

www.cambridge.org
Information on this title: www.cambridge.org/9781009454056

DOI: 10.1017/9781009122825

First published 2023

A catalogue record for this publication is available from the British Library

ISBN 978-1-009-45405-6 Hardback
ISBN 978-1-009-11408-0 Paperback
ISSN 2398-4031 (online)
ISSN 2514-3816 (print)

Representation and Taxation in the American South 1820–1910

Elements in Political Economy

DOI: 10.1017/9781009122825
First published online: October 2023

Jeffrey L. Jensen
New York University–Abu Dhabi

Giuliana Pardelli
New York University–Abu Dhabi

Jeffrey F. Timmons
New York University–Abu Dhabi

Author for correspondence: Jeffrey L. Jensen, jeffrey.jensen@nyu.edu

Abstract: We explain and document state-level fiscal developments in American Southern states from 1820 to 1910, focusing on their main source of revenue, progressive property taxes borne primarily by economic elites. The fourteen states in our analysis were characterized by severe economic exploitation of the enslaved and later politically repressed African-descended population by a small rural elite, who dominated the region both politically and economically. While rural elites are thought to be especially resistant to taxation, we offer a set of conditions that explains the emergence of progressive taxation and provides a coherent account of the fiscal development of these states over this period. Using an original, archival data set of annual tax revenues and select expenditure items, we show that the economic interests of these rural elites and the extent of their formal (over)representation played a critical role in shaping the observed fiscal patterns within and across Southern states over this period. This title is also available as Open Access on Cambridge Core.

The appendix for this Element can be found online at:
www.cambridge.org/Jensen

Keywords: political economy, rural elites, public goods, political inequality, property taxation

ISBNs: 9781009454056 (HB), 9781009114080 (PB), 9781009122825 (OC)
ISSNs: 2398-4031 (online), 2514-3816 (print)

Contents

A further Online Appendix can be accessed at
www.cambridge.org/Jensen_online_appendices

1 Political and Fiscal Development in the American South

1.1 Introduction

The story of the American South as an unequal, politically repressive, violent, exploitative, and backward society has been widely told.[1] Yet the fiscal history of this region over the long run has never been thoroughly examined. This Element fills this void. We study the evolution of political institutions and public finances across Southern states from 1820 to the eve of the adoption of the federal income tax in 1913 and the onset of World War I. The beginning of this period saw the rising use of enslaved labor to grow the cash crops demanded by rapidly industrializing Western economies, which led to the enrichment of a relatively small planter elite. The second half of this period witnessed the destruction of chattel slavery with the Confederacy's defeat in the American Civil War, the federal government's attempt to "reconstruct" the political systems of these states with the extension of suffrage to the newly emancipated, and the ultimate removal of these rights through the use of extensive violence. The period ends with the creation of the "One-Party South," which resulted in the continued political domination by a small elite well into the mid-twentieth century. As we will show, these momentous political and economic developments altered the power and preferences of the South's rural elites, setting in motion major changes in fiscal systems across and within states.

In seeking to explain and document the within- and cross-state fiscal patterns over this ninety-year period, we focus primarily on property taxes. Not only did property taxes comprise the vast majority of tax revenues in each of the fourteen states over this period, but they were borne most heavily by the same landed elites who dominated Southern politics. We have a secondary focus on alternative forms of tax revenue and on key investment-related expenditures, notably education and railroads. Taken together, these variables capture the most important elements of state-level finances in the American South during this period.

This Element has several key distinguishing features. First, we adopt a theoretically driven approach, building on a growing literature in political economy that seeks to explain variation across the world in taxation and state capacity (Meltzer and Richard 1981; Boix 2003; Sokoloff and Zolt 2006; Scheve and Stasavage 2010; Besley and Persson 2011; Ansell and Samuels 2014; Scheve and Stasavage 2016; Dincecco 2017; Beramendi, Dincecco, and Rogers 2019;

---

[1] See, for instance, among countless others, Kousser (1974); Wright (1978); Key (1984); Fogel (1994); Tolnay and Beck (1995); Ransom and Sutch (2001); Perman (2003); Einhorn (2006); Alston and Ferrie (2007); Margo (2007); Valelly (2009); McCurry (2012); Foner (2014); Bateman, Katznelson, and Lapinski (2018).

Suryanarayan and White 2021). While providing a parsimonious account of state-level finances is challenging due to the substantial heterogeneity across and within states throughout this period, we contend that a *fiscal-exchange* lens, focusing on the preferences and power of the landed elite, can help illuminate the historical record. The fiscal-exchange tradition posits that the most efficient, sustainable means of raising revenue is for states to trade services and goods for taxes, as long as three assumptions hold. First, collecting taxes purely through force is costly. Second, citizens are willing to accept taxes commensurate with coveted services – that is, they engage in what Levi (1988) called quasi-voluntary compliance. Third, commitment mechanisms – e.g., political representation via assemblies or political parties – ensure taxpayers that their money will be spent appropriately. The fiscal-exchange tradition thus links quasi-voluntary tax compliance to spending through formal representation, and argues that deviations from such an arrangement are likely to generate significant resistance and attempts to change the institutions that govern representation and fiscal policy.

We extend this framework to outline the conditions under which rural elites in an agricultural setting characterized by high levels of inequality and labor coercion would support or reject progressive taxation, and explain why they could not impose onerous taxes on other groups in society, notably low-income Whites. Given the agrarian structure of the Southern state economies and the concentration of assets and income in the hands of the plantation class, rural elites constituted the most obvious potential source of government revenue during the nineteenth century. As such, their willingness to comply with tax demands would determine in substantial part the amount of taxes raised, the costs of enforcement, and the sustainability of the fiscal pathway. Specifically, we argue that rural elites will support taxation on themselves and build fiscal capacity under three conditions. The first key driver is exclusive political control. If rural elites control politics in the present period and this control is likely to persist into the future, their willingness to increase taxation on themselves rises. Political control in the present period is necessary, as this determines how state fiscal resources are spent. Future control is also critical, as tax capacity, once established, can have a long half-life (D'arcy and Nistotskaya 2018). Without the expectation of future control, elites fear increasing the state's ability to extract, as power over taxation and spending could shift toward social groups with different preferences (e.g., urban residents or lower-income voters). Yet these two conditions are not sufficient on their own. We argue that in addition to political control, both in the present and into the future, rural elites must have demand for collective goods that will benefit their economic interests and are difficult to provision privately. By contrast, agricultural elites will seek to stymie progressive taxation under most other circumstances—i.e., when they are out of power or their dominance is contested, when there is uncertainty over future political control, or when demand for collective goods is weak or fragmented.

Explaining when and why rural elites accept self-taxation (and refrain from coercive taxation of others) adds fresh insights to the rich literature about the rise and fall of progressive taxes and the role of various elites in driving changes in fiscal systems. The existing literature has shown that rural elites may actively undermine the capacity for progressive taxation when power is uncertain or contested (Suryanarayan and White 2021); that rural elites may support progressive taxation when they can pass the burden onto emerging competitors, notably the manufacturing sector (Mares and Queralt 2015; Mares and Queralt 2020); and that *urban* elites may accept progressive taxes on themselves when they desire spending on human capital that will facilitate industrialization (Beramendi et al. 2019; Hollenbach 2021). The prevailing view, however, is that rural elites generally oppose fiscal extraction, especially when the burden could fall on them, and that polities controlled by rural elites eschew investments in fiscal capacity and adopt regressive tax systems (e.g., Lizzeri and Persico 2004; Galor and Moav 2006; Galor, Moav, and Vollrath 2009; Baten and Hippe 2018; Beramendi et al. 2019; Hollenbach 2021).[2]

Our analysis thus offers a nuanced challenge to existing accounts using an unlikely case, and also contributes several ideas to the fiscal-exchange literature – notably that quasi-voluntary compliance by rural elites rests on exclusive political control in the present and into the future. Specifically, we argue that merely having political representation in the present period, the standard minimal threshold for fiscal bargains, is insufficient, suggesting that high rural elite taxation is incompatible with shared state control. Second, instead of an exchange between rulers and economic elites over taxation and representation, we consider the consequences for taxation when the rulers and the primary target for taxation – due to their control of society's resources/assets – are the same. Although coercive taxation of non-elite groups by elites remains an

---

[2] According to Moore (2008, p. 44), for example, coercive extraction of the poor (rather than the wealthy) has been especially likely to emerge historically in agrarian societies where ruling elites "are unrestrained by their subjects (or alternative centres of power) and have no compelling reasons to seek broad support," features characterizing the US South during much of the period on which we focus. Furthermore, based on the specific conditions highlighted by several extant theories—e.g., the timing of industrialization for Beramendi et al. (2019, p. 50) and the extent of industrial political power for Hollenbach (2021, pp. 9–10) – indeed, the American South, which was a late industrializer without a politically powerful industrial class, would constitute an unlikely case of progressive taxation and increased government spending. One case, obviously, does not make or break a theory.

option in these settings, collecting taxes from low-income groups in agrarian economies tends to be costly and conflictual and to produce a low "tax take" (Moore 2008). Thus, rural elites interested in the provision of capital intensive public goods have incentives to refrain from imposing excessive tax burdens on other social groups if doing so has the potential to stimulate rebellion, exit, or demands for representation that could upend their exclusive control – especially if the tax yield would be low.

Critically, the South's rural elites were neither benevolent, nor did their actions trigger widely shared long-run development. They increased taxation on themselves to fund public spending that would benefit them disproportionately, rather than to provide public goods that would improve broader welfare or generate long-term development. The coexistence in the American South of greater investments in state capacity in the absence of broad-based development is consistent with claims found elsewhere (e.g., Queralt 2017).

The second key distinguishing feature of this Element is the abundance of original, archival data upon which it rests. We collected a nearly complete data set of annual state tax revenues, including specifically the amount of property taxes, for each state between 1820 and 1910. We complement these data with several additional measures, including the amount of regressive poll taxes levied for each state and ad valorem property tax rates over the same period. For a subset of states, we are also able to test whether rural elites "passed on" taxation by decomposing the share of property taxes levied on each sector (e.g., rural vs. urban). We also have the amount of substate (county, municipal, etc.) property taxes levied once every ten years between 1860 and 1910. This allows us to test whether there was substitution between state and substate taxes that could weaken our argument. Finally, we have data for key expenditure items, notably education and railroads. The comprehensive nature of our data not only allows us to test our argument vis-à-vis other arguments, but presents for the first time a relatively complete picture of Southern fiscal history at the state level over this period.[3]

Using these data and three distinct temporal shocks to the political institutions of Southern states, we find substantial support for our argument. In the prewar period between roughly 1820 and the early 1840s, we observe relatively low progressive taxation across all of these states. Yet the onset of a boom in international demand for Southern cash crops such as cotton, which increased the demand for land to be cultivated, combined with technological improvements in railroads that could unlock millions of acres of land that was far

---

[3] The primary existing data set of Southern state-level taxation by Sylla, Legler, and Wallis (1993) is appreciably less complete, particularly in the prewar era.

from navigable water, substantially increased the demand from Southern slave-holders for the construction of railroads – collective goods. We show that the shock had differential effects depending on the extent of planter control: only in states in which contemporary *and* future slaveholder political control was higher – due to legislative malapportionment that persistently overrepresented highly enslaved counties – did property taxes, which fell overwhelmingly on slaveholders, rise substantially. We show that these states also allocated significantly more state financing toward railroads and as a result constructed substantially more miles of railroad track. Importantly, rural elites in malapportioned states did not impose higher taxes on poorer Whites to finance state expansion.

The second period, Reconstruction (1867–77), was marked by emancipation from slavery, the extension of the franchise to all adult male former slaves, and its enforcement by Congress in the aftermath of the Civil War: the victorious federal government used the US Army to register Black voters and uphold their newly granted political rights. The presence of the Army, particularly in plantation areas, allowed for the imposition of higher property taxes, triggering a significant backlash against the fiscal policies and political institutions that facilitated such extraction (Foner 2014; Logan 2020; Suryanarayan and White 2021). However, the short-run fiscal effects of the federal intervention were substantial, especially in places where rural elites' formal political representation was disproportionately small. Progressive taxes rose the most in places where rural elites had the least political recourse for resisting taxation due to federal protection of Black voters and officeholders – that is, where the US military limited Southern elites' ability to use their disproportionate de facto power to prevent the expanded electorate from levying and collecting large amounts of progressive taxation. Property taxes rose the least in the four Southern states that were not occupied by federal troops.

The Reconstruction Southern tax boom lasted only as long as the federal intervention, which eroded across these states until finally ending with the Compromise of 1877. Once the federal government stopped subsidizing the costs of enforcing these policy changes, taxes across all of the previously occupied states converged to a lower level. In the absence of a powerful external enforcer, and facing intense political contestation, rural elites began to effectively curtail progressive taxation.

The third and final burst of property taxes occurred at the beginning of the "Jim Crow" period (circa 1890), during which eleven of the fourteen states adopted suffrage restrictions that disenfranchised their Black populations and some low-income Whites. With the decline in political contestation and rural elites once more gaining a firm control over state politics, the prospects of present and future cross-class and cross-race redistribution declined, and elite taxes increased – as did spending on selective public goods, such as universities. In the states without voting restrictions, by contract, property taxes and higher education spending lagged. Once again, rural elites in more protected political positions did not impose higher taxes on poorer Whites to finance state expansion.

In short, we contend, Southern fiscal development during this period largely reflects the power and preferences of the plantation class, whose members embraced progressive taxation when and where they wanted collective goods and had a secure grip on power but behaved contrastingly toward property taxes in circumstances where their dominance was contested.

This Element makes several contributions to at least two literatures. First, it contributes to the political economy of taxation literature by identifying precise and simple conditions that facilitate taxation of the rural rich, by the rural rich, and for the rural rich. Our framework not only establishes a higher minimal threshold for a bargain to emerge between rural elites and rulers than one commonly finds in the fiscal-exchange literature; it also suggests that some bargains may preclude others, making control of the state zero-sum. Second, it makes an important contribution to the historical American political economy literature. For one, our framework provides important analytical insights that distinguish our work from other explanations of Southern taxation, even those focusing on smaller, specific periods of time (Seligman 1969; Wallis 2000; Einhorn 2006). More broadly – and while much is known about individual Southern states, time periods, and particular dimensions of fiscal development – to our knowledge no work has tried to explain Southern fiscal developments across these fourteen states for this length of time, nor has any study drawn upon a nearly as complete annual data set of state taxation, or tried to put together both the revenue and spending sides of government accounts for each Southern state over these three different eras. Furthermore, the fact that our long-run analysis leverages exogenous shocks and considerable variation in both the input and output variables should lend confidence to the inferences.

This Element proceeds as follows. We begin with a brief historical overview of this period. In Section 2, we outline a theoretical framework for understanding Southern taxation and situate this within the existing literature on the political economy of taxation. In Section 3, we describe our data collection efforts and resulting data set in detail. In Section 4, we examine the prewar period (1820–60). We follow this in Section 5 by examining the postwar period (1868–1910).

1.2 Historical Context

The fourteen states that comprise our study are not called Southern states due simply to their geographic position relative to other states that made up the United States. Rather, their primary defining feature between the seventeenth and mid-twentieth centuries was the reliance on and exploitation of enslaved and later politically repressed agricultural laborers who descended from Africans brought against their will to the British North American colonies by a relatively small White rural elite.[4] While slavery was legal in each of the thirteen British colonies on the eve of the American Revolution (1775–83), only in the Southern coastal colonies from Maryland to Georgia was a quarter to half of the population enslaved (1790 Census).[5] As the US territory expanded westward and new states were admitted to the Union, slavery thrived in the Southern states, especially with the invention of the cotton gin in 1793 and the massive increase in international demand for cotton from industrializing Europe. At the same time, each Northern state successively abolished or severely restricted slavery.[6] By 1850, 99 percent of the approximately 3.2 million enslaved people lived in the fourteen states we study. Table 1 reports key variables of interest for each state and period of our study between 1820 and 1910. Column 1 reports the share of the total population who were enslaved in 1820, the first year of our study, and column 2 shows the same in 1860, the year before the American Civil War began.

Whereas slavery was the main defining feature of the Southern economy and society, two other crucial features need highlighting.[7] First, the South, especially the more heavily enslaved states that later formed the Confederacy, was overwhelmingly rural and agrarian. Figure 1 provides a comparative perspective, showing the urbanization rate every ten years between 1820 and 1910 for the US South, the first fifteen Northern US states, England and Wales, and the

---

[4] Despite federal-level legality until 1808, most slaves brought to the United States arrived prior to the American Revolution.

[5] These five states contained roughly 93 percent of the country's total enslaved population in 1790.

[6] While many people remained enslaved in Northern states, antislavery and gradual abolition laws were adopted by each of the original Northern states by 1804. The Northwest Ordinance of 1787 prohibited slavery in the Northwest Territory – the area that would become the states of Illinois, Indiana, Michigan, Minnesota, Ohio, and Wisconsin. The corresponding Southwest Ordinance of 1790 permitted slavery in the territories south of the Ohio River (Alabama, Kentucky, Mississippi, and Tennessee).

[7] By 1860, the enslaved made up more than half of the Southern agricultural labor force (Ransom 2001) and accounted for nearly half of all tangible Southern wealth (Wright 2022). On the importance of slavery for the prewar Southern economy, see, e.g., Ransom (2001), González, Marshall, and Naidu (2017), and Wright (2022).

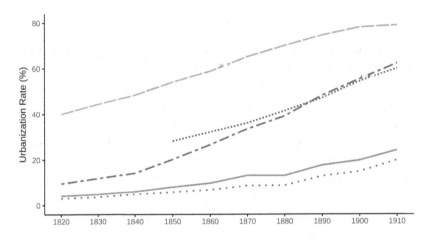

· · Confederate States (11) —— South (14) ···· German Empire ▪ ▪ North (15) —— England/Wales

Figure 1 Urbanization rate across regions, 1820–1910

German Empire over the same period.[8] The Southern urbanization rate in 1910 is roughly half the value of England's in 1820, and just barely above the US North's figure for 1850. Figure 2 shows the agricultural share of output (comprising agricultural and manufacturing activities). The share of manufacturing output in the average Northern state in 1850 exceeds the same share in the average Southern state in 1910.

Second, Southern states were characterized by extreme levels of economic inequality, as the ownership of the enslaved was heavily concentrated in a small minority. The average enslaver in 1860, for example, had approximately fourteen times the wealth of the average non-slaveholder (Wright 1978, p. 36), and the Southern wealth Gini coefficient was estimated to be 0.71 (Ransom 2001, pp. 63–64).[9] Furthermore, due to the low levels of economic integration between the high-enslaved ("lowland") and low-enslaved ("highland/upland") areas across the South (Wright 1978, p. 39), the economic spillovers of

---

[8] The urbanization rate is the share of total population living in municipalities of at least 2,500 inhabitants in the United States (Census, 1820–1910), and England and Wales (Law 1967), and 2,000 people in the German Empire (Reulecke 1977). Note that the German Empire had a lower urbanization rate than Prussia, while the eleven Confederate states had lower urbanization rates than the fourteen states we classify as Southern.

[9] Using the 1860 Census, we estimate that 10 percent of the South's adult White males owned approximately 90 percent of the slaves. The share of adult White males who owned at least twenty slaves, the traditional definition of a planter, was below 8 percent in every state. If we use adult White males as a rough approximation of the electorate in each state, in no state did more than 40 percent of the voters own at least one slave.

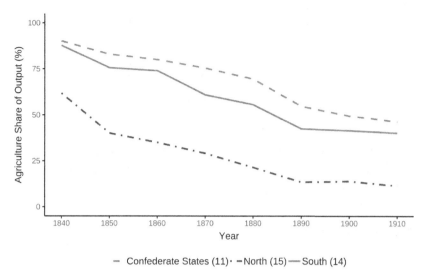

— Confederate States (11)· − North (15) — South (14)

Figure 2 Agriculture share of output (agriculture and manufacturing), 1840–1910

Southern slavery were fairly low to most of the majority nonslaveowner White population.

Not only was economic inequality between enslaver and non-enslaver Whites high, poor Whites also experienced substantial political inequality as a result of slavery. While enslavers were unlikely to have ever comprised a majority of the adult White male population in any Southern colony or state, the historical record leaves little doubt that slaveholders dominated colonial and later state politics (Green 1966; Wooster 1969, 1975; Johnson 1999; McCurry 2012; Thornton 2014; Merritt 2017; Chacón and Jensen 2020c). Their dominance stemmed from substantial advantages in not only de facto but de jure power[10] – for example, during colonial times they used their dominance to structure political institutions, including the malapportionment of state legislatures to systematically overrepresent districts with greater enslaved density (Green 1966; Chacón and Jensen 2020a).

Enslaver dominance of Southern state governments was critical because states played the primary role in the promotion of economic development and the provision of public goods in the prewar period (Wallis 2000; Wallis and Weingast 2018). Thus the promotion of economic development, including

---

[10] Acemoglu and Robinson (2006, pp. 325–326) define de jure power "as the political power allocated by political institutions (such as constitutions or electoral systems)" and de facto power as something that "emerges from the ability to engage in collective action, or use brute force or other channels such as lobbying or bribery." In terms of the South, de facto power refers to what Donnelly (1965) called "the traditional powers of their planter oligarchy."

publicly supported systems of education and infrastructure, as well as the choice on the system of taxation to finance these public expenditures, was substantially influenced by a small rural elite.

The 1860 election of the Republican candidate, Abraham Lincoln, to the presidency led to the rapid secession of eleven Southern states and the formation of the Confederate States of America in February 1861.[11] The Confederacy's defeat in the American Civil War (1861–5) and the passage of the Thirteenth Amendment to the US Constitution, abolishing slavery, resulted in the permanent emancipation of nearly 4 million enslaved Southerners (out of a total population of roughly 12 million).

Congressional Republicans sought to use the South's defeat as an opportunity to transform each state's political system with the goal of diminishing the power of the small planter elite (Foner 2014).[12] With the passage of several Military Reconstruction Acts in 1867 and 1868, "radical Reconstruction" would entail the use of the military to register all adult Black males to vote and then protect their access to the ballot box in the ten Reconstruction states.[13] Furthermore, the passage of the Fourteenth and Fifteenth Amendments would, in principle, offer the recently enfranchised equal protection under the law, guaranteed citizenship, and the prohibition of racial disenfranchisement.

For a brief period, Southern politics was completely upended. Table 1, column 3 shows the share of each state's registered voters who were Black in 1867–8.[14] This led to the election for the first time in American history of thousands of Blacks to local, state, and federal office across the ten Reconstruction states (Foner 1993). There was a fundamental expansion in the role of the Southern state, especially with respect to public education. This fiscal expansion was financed primarily by raising property taxes that fell most heavily on the small, landed elite.[15]

---

[11] The original six Confederate states seceded by January 1861. Texas followed in March. The final four states that would make up the Confederacy joined after the attack on Fort Sumter in April made war an inevitability. The "border" slave states of Kentucky, Maryland, and Missouri ultimately remained in the Union.

[12] This was both because this elite was seen as dominating prewar federal politics – so called Slave Power – and because they hoped to create a competitive Southern Republican Party that could contest for federal office. Congressional Republicans did not want to cede the South to the Democratic Party, especially as the newly passed Fourteenth Amendment increased Southern representation with the removal of the three-fifths clause for federal apportionment.

[13] Congressional Reconstruction was the price to be readmitted to federal representation. The three border states never lost representation, and Tennessee had been readmitted in 1866.

[14] Black adult males comprised 40 percent or more of registered voters in ten of eleven states (Walton, Puckett, and Deskins 2012).

[15] As Foner (2014, p. 365) emphasizes, "Not only the scope of its activity, but the interests it aspired to serve distinguished the Reconstruction state from its predecessors and successors. ... All these activities inevitably entailed a dramatic growth in the cost of government."

The rising tax burden quickly emerged as a focal point for Reconstruction's opponents. In several states, Democratic leaders organized taxpayers' conventions, whose supporters demanded a reduction in spending and called for a return to rule by men of property – which entailed denying Blacks, as well as some Whites, any role in Southern public affairs (Foner 2014). From the outset, this largely elite-driven backlash against Radical Republican rule used highly organized terrorist groups, such as the Ku Klux Klan, to restore Democratic Party rule and limit Black political power. Despite the promise to use the federal military to enforce these newly granted civil and political rights, the occupation was never extensive enough to protect a largely rural Black population, thinly distributed across the vast South.[16] Furthermore, with western expansion making greater demands on federal resources, the size of the occupation decreased throughout the period of Congressional Reconstruction (1867–77). The extensive use of violence eventually resulted in the return to power of the Democratic Party, termed "Redemption" by the conservative elites who had been restored to office.[17] Federal military enforcement of Black political rights ended with the so-called Compromise of 1877.[18]

While the end of Reconstruction saw Black political power fall substantially, the political control of the planter class was by no means uncontested. For one, Blacks formally retained the right to vote and therefore remained a threat to the political dominance of Southern Democratic elites (Kousser 1974; Perman 2003; Valelly 2009). In terms of future power, the possibility remained that the federal government would intervene on behalf of Black voters. Moreover, elections continued to be highly contested affairs: the period between 1880 and 1900 saw opposition parties routinely win more than a third of the state legislative seats, and non-Democratic Party candidates often won more than 40 percent of the popular vote for governor (Dubin 2007, 2010).

These working-class electoral threats to Democratic Party rule largely ceased between 1889 and 1907 with the adoption of suffrage restrictions, such as poll taxes and literacy tests, in eleven Southern states, which had the consequence

---

[16] Chacón, Jensen, and Yntiso (2021) demonstrate that Black state legislators were much more likely to be elected in counties occupied by federal troops than otherwise similar unoccupied counties. As the occupation declined, fewer Black politicians were elected and thousands were assassinated (Egerton 2014).

[17] While the full extent of the violence used against Blacks during Reconstruction is unknown, it has been estimated that more than 50,000 were murdered, with possibly a third of these murders being politically motivated (Egerton 2014).

[18] The presidential election of 1876 erupted into a constitutional crisis when the pivotal electoral votes for Florida, Louisiana, and South Carolina were claimed by both parties. While the details are still in dispute, the resolution of this crisis possibly involved Southern support for the Republican candidate, Hayes, as a trade for the removal of the few remaining federal troops supporting Reconstruction.

of formally disenfranchising most Black voters. At the same time, the threat of federal intervention on behalf of Black rights receded substantially after 1890. The defeat of the Lodge Federal Elections Bill of 1890, which would have provided for the federal regulation of congressional elections, ended Congress' efforts to protect Southern Black voters until the 1960s. That states would be largely left to their own devices was largely confirmed in May 1896 and April 1898, when the Supreme Court handed down two decisions that ratified developments in the South. *Plessy v. Ferguson* (1896) confirmed the federal government's inability to protect individual rights within the states, and *Williams v. Mississippi* (1898) removed any remaining uncertainty that the methods of disfranchisement employed in the South would be declared unconstitutional (Perman 2003). These factors contributed to the creation of the "One-Party South," which would reign through much of the twentieth century.

Table 1 shows some key demographic and political features of this final period of our study – the onset of "Jim Crow" (1889–1910). Column 4 reports the share of each state's population who were Black in 1900,[19] and columns 7 and 8 show the date and type of suffrage restrictions adopted.

2 Theoretical Framework

2.1 The Existing Literature

We know that some polities are better at raising revenue than others and that the incidence of taxation varies significantly across space and time. The existing scholarship on this topic is sufficiently broad and multifaceted that our coverage of the literature will necessarily be limited. Generally speaking, extant theories emphasize the role of four broad factors to explain tax patterns, particularly the emergence of progressive taxation: temporary contextual factors, especially war (e.g., Tilly 1975; Scheve and Stasavage 2010), structural conditions that determine actor incentives as well as the technical feasibility of particular fiscal arrangements, such as geography or the structure of the economy (Moore 2008; Ross 2015; Mayshar, Moav, and Neeman 2017), the specific constellation of social and political groups, such as ethnic or class solidarity or the nature of political coalitions (e.g., Lieberman 2003; Ansell and Samuels 2014; Saylor 2014; Mares and Queralt 2015, 2020; Beramendi et al. 2019; Suryanarayan and White 2021), and the institutions that govern the relationship between citizens and the state (e.g., Levi 1988; North and Weingast 1989; Stasavage 2007; Timmons 2010). Additionally, within each of these categories,

---

[19] Approximately 90 percent of the almost 9 million total Black population in the United States in 1900 still resided in these fourteen states.

Table 1 The fourteen Southern states, 1820–1910

	Enslaved pop. share 1820 (%) (1)	Enslaved pop. share 1860 (%) (2)	Black share reg. voters 1868 (%) (3)	Black pop. share 1900 (%) (4)	Prewar malapportioned state (5)	Reconstruction state (6)	Type of suffrage restriction (7)	Year enacted (8)
Alabama	33	45	63	45	0	1	LT, PT	1901
Arkansas		26	35	28	0	1	PT	1892
Florida		44	58	44	1	1	PT	1889
Georgia	44	44	50	47	1	1	LT, PT	1906*
Kentucky	23	19		13	0	0	None	
Louisiana	45	47	65	47	1	1	LT, PT	1898
Maryland	26	13		20	1	0	None	
Mississippi	44	55	56	59	0	1	LT, PT	1890
Missouri	15	10		5	0	0	None	
N. Carolina	32	33	41	33	1	1	LT, PT	1900
S. Carolina	51	57	63	58.4	1	1	LT, PT	1895
Tennessee	19	25	40	24	0	0	PT	1889
Texas		30	46	22	0	1	PT	1902
Virginia	40	31	47	36	1	1	LT, PT	1901

Note: Arkansas (1836), Florida (1845), and Texas (1845) were admitted as states after 1820. LT = Literacy Test. PT = Poll Tax. *Georgia enacted the literacy test in 1906 and the poll tax in 1877. Sources: Kousser (1974), Valelly (2009), Walton et al. (2012, Table 13.9); US Census (1820, 1860, and 1900).

there are two basic approaches for explaining variation in the form of taxation: the *coercive approach*, which underscores the extractive power of governments to impose taxes regardless of the preferences of taxpayers, and the *fiscal contract* perspective, which emphasizes mutually agreed-upon bargains between state leaders and resource holders.

Coercion-based models of taxation are predicated on the absence of a negotiated exchange between state leaders and social actors: taxpayers lack representation, and there is no guarantee that policy decisions will reflect their preferences. Coercive extraction explicitly allows for a disjuncture between the incidence of taxes and spending – that is, for relatively unfettered redistribution.[20] Much of the recent work focusing on elite taxation follows a coercion-based logic.[21] The canonical median-voter model (Meltzer and Richard 1981) and its myriad offshoots (e.g., Boix 2003; Acemoglu et al. 2015), for example, contend that elites will be taxed more heavily in democratic societies, particularly when inequality is high. More recent scholarship has instead stressed various forms of intra-elite conflict as a potential trigger for progressive direct taxation, in which one elite group successfully shifts the tax burden onto another elite group in an effort to restrict the latter's de facto political or economic power (Mares and Queralt 2015, 2020).

By contrast, contractual models of taxation posit the existence of a negotiated exchange based on mutual interests of governments and social actors in which taxes are traded for goods and services. According to these models, people will engage in what Levi (1988) called *quasi-voluntary compliance* when public spending reflects their preferences. Spending that deviates from taxpayer desires, by contrast, engenders resistance to taxes and the political arrangement that generated them.[22] Mechanisms of voice and accountability solve commitment problems between rulers and taxpayers, facilitating tax increases and investments in fiscal capacity (Bates and Lien 1985; North and Weingast

---

[20] Notably, here "redistribution" encompasses both those cases in which the rich are taxed more heavily and government revenues are spent on universal public goods or transfers to poorer citizens, as well as those in which elites are the ones benefiting from regressive transfers at the expense of other social groups – much like the "redistributive state" conceived by Polanyi (1944) and modeled by Besley and Persson (2011).

[21] See Acemoglu et al. (2015) and Scheve and Stasavage (2017) for recent surveys.

[22] The historical record is replete with narratives linking coercive and redistributive taxation with revolt or rebellion. The slogan "no taxation without representation," for example, animated the American Revolution. David Ramsay, one of the earliest historians of the American Revolution, wrote that the colonists' uprising against a small tax on tea was motivated by the belief that they "could not be compelled to pay any taxes, nor be bound by any laws, but such as had been granted or enacted by the consent of themselves, or of their representatives" (1789: 20). Similarly, Thomas Millard (1926) commented that Chinese "revolutions start with the tax collector" (in Bernstein and Lü 2003, p. 252).

1989).[23] Because tax collection costs are endogenous to how governments raise revenue and how they spend it, high levels of cross-group redistribution (e.g., from rich to poor and vice versa) is difficult to sustain, barring some type of compensation along the lines identified by Lieberman (2003) and Scheve and Stasavage (2016). These authors show that redistribution can emerge in equilibrium as a side payment for ethnic solidarity (e.g., in Lieberman, a cross-class alliance among Whites to repress Blacks in South Africa), or for the differential costs of war (e.g., in Scheve and Stasavage, the wealthy disproportionately fund warfare while the masses bear the brunt of the fighting). In both cases, taxes on the rich represent a form of compensatory redistribution tied together by shared identities and/or sacrifices.

Even though trading services for revenue is a more efficient and sustainable means of raising revenue than coercive extraction, a fiscal contract between elites and rulers may not always emerge. Negotiated exchanges are more attractive in the presence of specific conditions: namely, when members of (potential) taxpaying groups have similar material interests and policy preferences;[24] the public sector has a comparative advantage in the production of the desired collective good or service (Levi 1988); and there are commitment mechanisms ensuring taxpayers that their money will be well spent (Bates and Lien 1985; Levi 1988; Dincecco 2011; Garfias 2019; Flores-Macías 2022). Commitment mechanisms include assemblies (North and Weingast 1989; Hoffman and Norberg 1994) that guarantee at least a voice, if not an explicit veto, over fiscal decisions, and political parties (Stasavage 2007; Timmons 2010), who act as agents for groups of taxpayers. Beyond the factors affecting the likelihood of emergence of fiscal contracts, there are also contextual elements that can influence the parameters of these bargains, some of which we develop in what follows.

Changes in the economy, notably industrialization, have been associated with increased prospects for progressive taxation. One reoccurring claim is that urban elites benefit more from public expenditures than rural elites (e.g., Lizzeri and Persico 2004; Beramendi et al. 2019; Hollenbach 2021): spending on education, sanitation, and infrastructure raises returns to industrial capital and draws labor to cities, potentially harming agrarian interests (e.g., Baten

---

[23] Many early modern representative institutions emerged, in fact, as part of an explicit bargain in which the elite agreed to provide tax revenue in return for representation in assemblies, thereby creating an explicit link between taxation and representation (Dincecco 2011).

[24] One finds quasi-voluntary tax relationships between economic elites and government for a variety of specific goods and services, including security or defense (Scheve and Stasavage 2010; Dincecco 2011; Flores-Macías 2022), property rights (Timmons 2005), and firm/sector-specific protections (Queralt 2017).

and Hippe 2018; Galor et al. 2009). Hence, rising urban elites may be willing to shoulder a higher tax burden through progressive direct taxation in order to fund public goods that increase industrial output (Ansell and Samuels 2014; Beramendi et al. 2019; Hollenbach 2021). However, the spending pressures caused by industrialization do not always result in the expansion of taxation. Rather, an increase in tax revenue is possible only where new capitalist elites can translate their economic power into political influence (e.g., Emmenegger, Leemann, and Walter 2021).[25]

Likewise, the nature of the tax base may influence the incentives for both rulers and taxpayers to bargain around exchanging representation for resources. Actors with more mobile assets, for example, are more likely to be granted government benefits and a voice in government decisions in exchange for revenue (Bates and Lien 1985), while actors with less mobile assets, notably agriculture and mining, may find themselves held hostage: the fixed nature of their assets means they cannot withdraw if the exchange with the state becomes unfavorable (Zolberg 1980). Historically, in fact, rural elites have been rather successful at blocking unilateral extraction on the part of the state – a capability attributed to both de jure political institutions that overweight their preferences and de facto forms of power that impede meaningful political change (Acemoglu and Robinson 2006; Alston and Ferrie 2007; Ziblatt 2009; Albertus and Menaldo 2014).

The emergence of fiscal bargains also depends, in part, on the availability of alternative sources of revenue. Rulers enjoying large nontax incomes from natural resource rents, access to loans, large inflows of aid, or the exploitation of state property – such as railways, post offices, or mines – may be less compelled to exchange representation for resources (as summarized in Ross [2015]).

Finally, another relevant strand in the literature explains the rise and fall of progressive taxation as a function of ethnic solidarity in a context of salient class and racial cleavages – conditions that clearly characterized the American South. Lieberman (2003), for example, argues that the political exclusion of Blacks in apartheid South Africa prompted the emergence of a cross-class coalition among Whites in which progressive taxes and spending went hand

---

[25] Mares and Queralt, by contrast, argue that progressive income taxes were more likely to be adopted where the power of "landowning elites was severely threatened by the rise of a new economic elite linked to the emerging manufacturing sector. Anticipating a future decline in economic power, politicians representing the interests of landowning elites regarded the income tax as a tool that could rebalance some of these economic losses by imposing a higher tax burden on the industrial sector" (2015, p. 1976). While Mares and Queralt (2015, 2020) view elite competition and rural political power as the driving forces behind burden-shifting and coercive taxation, we will argue that more complete and secure rural elite control (in effect, the absence of competition) drives contractual self-taxation.

in hand. Suryanarayan and White (2021), by contrast, set forth the conditions that generate intra-ethnic solidarity with the aim of undermining taxation and bureaucratic capacity. Specifically, they contend that the expansion of the franchise to African Americans in the United States threatened the prevailing vertical racial order and gave rise to a cross-class coalition among Whites that weakened taxation and state capacity where the legacy of slavery was strongest. In particular, the authors claim that intra-White inequality was a key determinant of tax patterns following the Civil War. Our empirical analysis will engage with Lieberman's alternative explanation and address the threat to inference posed by the potential omitted variable highlighted by Suryanarayan and White.

Missing in this rich literature, however, is an explanation for (and examples of) rural elites' support for (self-)taxation in contexts where they already have representation, and indeed may be the uncontested incumbent power holders with no challengers on the horizon, something our analysis provides.

2.2 The Argument

We argue that three conditions are pivotal to determining rural elites' preferences over public finance and, in particular, their willingness to tax themselves when they are in power. First, rural elites must value some "public good" that the state can produce at a lower cost than they can provide privately.[26] While obtaining benefits from spending is a necessary condition for self-taxation, as others have highlighted (e.g., Timmons 2005; Beramendi et al. 2019; Hollenbach 2021), we claim it is not sufficient.

Second, unlike other groups, rural elites must have relatively exclusive control over, if not an outright monopoly on, political power, rather than just representation. Their reluctance to accept taxes amidst shared governance stems from several factors. Their assets are highly specific, visible, not particularly mobile, and disproportionately valuable. They thus have fewer exit options and are more exposed to taxation and expropriation. Furthermore, their preferences over spending are often vastly different from that of other groups in society. Specific goods, such as public education, sanitation, or urban infrastructure, could undermine the economic system that undergirds their rent generation. Finally, because they are a numerically small group, many sets of voting rights can prove unfavorable. Given these characteristics, governing

---

[26] The term "public good" refers to a class of goods that are nonexcludable and nonrivalrous. "Impure" public goods fall somewhere between private goods and pure public goods. They might either be characterized by limited rivalry or feature some type of exclusion mechanism in their consumption. Although impure public goods may disproportionately benefit certain groups in society, they still produce positive externalities and are distinct from private goods.

coalitions may find it challenging to credibly commit to not expropriating rural elites, especially in the event of an exogenous shift in power.

Third, besides exclusive political control in the present, elites must believe that their power will remain unchallenged: assured future political dominance minimizes the chances that the enhanced extractive tools of the state will be used to expropriate their wealth later. Our logic is similar to that of Besley and Persson (2011), in that political stability lengthens rulers' time horizon. However, where their model predicts that stability leads to investments via taxation on non-ruling groups ("redistributive state"), our argument posits that when political elites are asset owners with strong demands for public goods, stability eliminates the commitment problem, paving the way to increase self-taxation.

In other words, rural elites may be less likely to rely on the state for collective goods and, as economic actors that derive power from the control of valuable economic resources that are especially vulnerable to taxation, they may be more attuned to time-consistency problems. However, if they desire public goods in which the state has a comparative advantage, and they feel secure about their monopoly on power, they have incentives to tax themselves.[27] These empirical conditions mean that rural elites' threshold for agreeing to voluntary taxation will be relatively high.

A corollary of our argument is that elites have self-enforcing incentives to refrain from imposing hefty taxes on other social groups, so long as such taxes could generate counter-reactions that might threaten their monopoly on power.[28] We contend that Southern elites did, in fact, face formidable technical and political barriers to shifting an increased burden onto other groups. First, the urban/manufacturing sector was small, even by the end of the period. At the same time, netting tax revenue from yeoman farmers and peasants is notoriously daunting (Moore 2008): the lack of formal records of economic transactions, the seasonality and instability of farm production, the generally low levels of cash income, and the paucity of wealth outside of the plantation economy meant, in all likelihood, that a considerable amount of revenue would have been absorbed by the collection costs.

Second, coercive taxation, especially if arbitrary and capricious, should stimulate tax resistance, migration toward less extortionate jurisdictions, demands

---

[27] Our argument does not presume that rural elites are homogeneous on all dimensions, but may require a minimal degree of consensus regarding the level and type of state-supplied public goods.

[28] The fact that elites eschewed taxation of other groups does not mean that they did not engage in other forms of coercive extraction. In fact, enslaved Blacks were seconded as labor for railroad construction in various places. Nonetheless, the extensive labor coercion Southern elites employed against Blacks was not fully fungible for capital-intensive goods.

for representation, and pressure to change the institutions that determine fiscal policies. Thanks to the work of historians (e.g., Foner 2014), and social scientists (e.g., Chacón and Jensen 2020b; Logan 2020; Suryanarayan and White 2021), we know that redistributive taxes and spending during Reconstruction generated a violent elite-led backlash that undermined the tax system by targeting the electoral and bureaucratic institutions from which it emerged.

Coercive taxation on non-elite groups in the South presented its own complications. First, non-elite Southern Whites were sufficiently mobile and numerous to pose problems if angered. Indeed, the threat of migration was not just hypothetical. According to the 1860 Census, approximately 25 percent of the Whites born in the original Southern states, as well as those born in later-admitted slave states, such as Alabama, Kentucky, and Tennessee, had migrated out of these states. Furthermore, outside of large cities, such as Baltimore, New Orleans, and St. Louis, Southern states received few European immigrants during the various waves of immigration. Out-migration of both Blacks and Whites accelerated after the Civil War, with White migration especially intense in the first two decades following the conflict. Second, anti-elite political movements were a recurring phenomenon (Kousser 1974; Hyman 1989; Hahn 2006; Gailmard and Jenkins 2018), which culminated in the 1880s and 1890s when populists threatened Democratic Party rule in many Southern states (e.g., Alabama, Arkansas, Georgia). Excessive taxes on lower-income Whites or urban areas could have enhanced prospects of a class-based Black-White alliance after the Civil War, which would have eroded uncontested planter political control. In fact, these are not mere conjectures: working-class Black-White coalitions did win control of state governments in Virginia (early 1880s) and North Carolina (mid-1890s) and fell just short in several other states (Perman 2003). In sum, in certain places and time periods, Southern rural elites had the capacity and motivation to embrace self-taxation; in other places and time periods, they had the incentive and power to fight redistributive taxes.

3 Data and Empirical Strategy

We created an original annual data set of state-level taxation between 1820 and 1910 across fourteen Southern states to assess our hypothesis about the relationship between rural elite power and fiscal outcomes.[29] We located auditor, comptroller, and US Treasury reports for as many years as possible from each state. We intentionally excluded the Civil War and pre-Congressional

---

[29] As shown in Table 1, Arkansas (1836), Florida (1845), and Texas (1845) were admitted as states after 1820.

Reconstruction years from 1861 to 1867.[30] With these years omitted and accounting for the three states that entered after 1820, our sample comprises 1,146 possible state-years. From these reports, we extracted the total tax revenues collected into the state treasury, as well as tax revenues by type. These include property taxes, poll taxes, occupation and licensing fees, business taxes (e.g., on banks and insurance companies), and miscellaneous taxes, such as those on the sale of liquor and fertilizer.

3.1 Property Taxes between 1820 and 1910

Our primary variable of interest is the annual amount of property taxes levied and collected. We focus on this particular tax for two reasons. First, property taxes accounted for the majority of tax revenues for most state-years in our data set, especially after 1840. In a sample of approximately 800 state-years in which we have both property taxes and total tax revenues, property taxes accounted for roughly 74 percent of total state tax revenues.[31] Second, unlike regressive taxation such as liquor taxes, poll (capitation) taxes, and occupational licenses, these taxes fell most heavily on the same small, rural, planter elite that dominated Southern politics (Wright 1978; Thornton 1982; Ransom and Sutch 2001). We provide additional support for this claim, as well as a short overview of property tax liabilities, assessment, and collection.

Property tax systems evolved considerably during the period under study. The systems that emerged during the colonial and early postindependence periods were rudimentary (Einhorn 2006; Rabushka 2010). While property taxes were a sizeable portion of tax revenues, they rarely entailed an attempt to assess systematically each individual household's value of real estate and personal property. Instead, certain taxable property (e.g., farm animals and equipment, slaves, etc.) was assessed on a fixed per-item basis, meaning that items with very different economic values could face similar liabilities. Land was typically assigned to a few categories based primarily on its geographic location (i.e., soil, access to navigable water, etc.) and then charged a differential per-acre rate.

Following developments that began in Missouri in the 1820s, Southern states began adopting property tax systems in which the same ad valorem rate (uniformity) was applied to all private property (universality). This entailed the creation of a much more sophisticated tax collection infrastructure that could

---

[30] In addition to the difficulty in locating reports for each state-year during this period, comparability across periods and non-Confederate states is further complicated by the Confederate states' use of their own (debased) currency.

[31] This is consistent with estimates Wallis (2000) offers for all US states in this period.

assess the value of all taxable property. As Einhorn (2006, p. 242) details, the transition to uniform property tax systems was politically contested, as rural elites (successfully) fought "to limit the taxes that majorities could impose on them."[32] By 1860, all fourteen states had adopted an ad valorem property tax system for land and other non-enslaved personal property and only five continued to use capitation taxes for slaves. The new state governments created by the Reconstruction Acts each adopted a uniform property tax system for all taxable property, and this system remained in place throughout the remainder of the period of our study.

As property tax systems became more sophisticated, and the structure of the economy developed, more classes of assets were included in assessed wealth. By the 1840s, most states included the value of money (deposits in banks), bonds (and to a lesser extent stocks), the value of commercial merchandise, and household items, such as jewelry, gold and silver watches, and furniture. In the postwar period, the property tax system enlarged to include the value of capital in banks, the assessed value of railroads, and manufacturing; there were even attempts to include intangible assets, such as patents and copyrights. Small exemptions (e.g., church property, the first $200–500, or 100 head of cattle) were common throughout the period.

The assessment of the value of taxable property was in the hands of local officials, and these valuations were used for property taxes at all levels (state, county, municipality, and special-purpose, such as school and levee districts). While local officials had the incentive to undervalue the assessments compared to true market values, the strategic under-assessment of property values was not a South-specific problem; it was endemic across the entire United States (e.g., Seligman 1969; Vollrath 2013).

3.1.1 Empirical Measures of Property Taxes

Our main measure of property taxes uses a combination of property taxes levied and collected. For the prewar period, the reports were much less detailed and few provided the amount of property taxes levied. Given the paucity of data on prewar property taxes levied (not to mention assessments of the value of taxable property), our prewar property taxes are primarily those collected into the treasury each year. For the postwar years, we generally use the amount of property taxes levied. This information is commonly provided in each report, and tables of annual property taxes levied for long periods (which increase our

---

[32] According to Einhorn (2006, p. 250), "Slaveholders were not always unwilling to pay taxes. Sometimes, they supported lavish spending for which they paid large parts of the tab. But slaveholders would not allow nonslaveholders to decide how to tax."

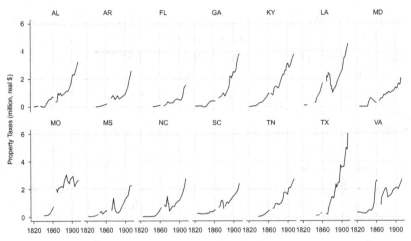

Figure 3 Total property taxes by state (million, real $), 1820–1910 three-year moving average

coverage) are often included. More importantly, it became typical that some state property taxes, especially those levied specifically for common schools (as pre-high school public schools were then called), were not received by the state treasury and therefore not recorded in our measure of property taxes collected. We think it is important to include all property taxes levied by the state government. We believe our measure of property taxes is comparable across states and periods, since we know of no instances in the prewar period in which state-levied property taxes did not go into the state treasury.

In general, we have excellent coverage across states and time in annual property taxes. For the 1,146 possible state-years in our sample, we have collected property taxes for 919 of them. For the eleven states that existed in 1820, there are 87 possible state-years each. We have at least 54 observations for each of them.[33] Unsurprisingly, the completeness of data improves over time. In the 1820s, we have property taxes for 45 of 110 possible state-years.[34] We have 64 of the possible 114 state-years in the 1830s. For the 1850s, we have 117 of 140 possible data points. We have 133 of 140 possible state-years in the last decade of our sample.

The period of our study, especially after the Panic of 1873, was characterized by substantial deflation. As a result, our measure of property taxes (as well as all

---

[33] We were able to locate only two years of property tax data before 1840 for Louisiana and none for Missouri and Tennessee. For states admitted after 1820, we have excellent coverage. We have 64 of 69 possible state-year observations for Arkansas (admitted in 1836), and 54 of 61 possible observations each for Florida and Texas (both admitted in 1845).

[34] We have three or fewer observations in the 1820s for Louisiana (2), Maryland (3), Missouri (0), and Tennessee (0).

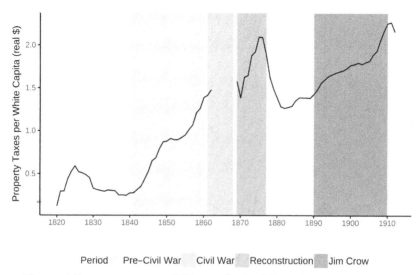

Figure 4 Property taxes per White capita (real $), 1820–1910 three-year moving average

variables collected in nominal dollars) is reported in deflated values.[35] Figure 3 shows the total property taxes in each state between 1820 and 1910. We smooth it using a three-year rolling average.

We normalize this measure of property taxes in two ways. First, we divide it by each state's White population. We use White population rather than total population because even in the post-emancipation period, Whites owned almost all of the taxable property in Southern states.[36] The denominator is created using census data for each decade from 1820 to 1910 and performing linear interpolation for the intervening years.

Figure 4 shows the average across these fourteen states for property taxes per White capita (PWC) from 1820 to 1910. Initially, property taxes PWC were low, especially in the 1830s. They rose rapidly between the early 1840s and the onset of the Civil War in 1861. We see that they continued to rise during Reconstruction only to decline significantly once Reconstruction ends. The post–Black disenfranchisement or Jim Crow period saw the resumption

---

[35] Source: www.minneapolisfed.org/about-us/monetary-policy/inflation-calculator/consumer-price-index-1800-.

[36] For instance, despite comprising nearly 50 percent of Georgia's population in 1890, Black Georgians owned less than 3 percent of the state's assessed taxable property wealth – i.e., paid less than 3 percent of the state's property taxes (*Report of the Comptroller-General, 1890*, pp. 4–5). Other states that provided information on taxable property by race (e.g., Arkansas, Louisiana) reported nearly identical proportions.

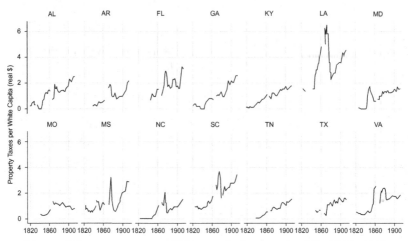

Figure 5 Property taxes per White capita by state (real $), 1820–1910

of rapidly rising property taxes PWC. Figure 5 shows the amount of property taxes PWC by state from 1820 and 1910.

Our second measure normalizes property taxes by the value of total agricultural and manufacturing output, as collected by each census between 1840 and 1910.[37] This attempts to measure taxes as a share of economic output.[38] As with the White population, we perform linear interpolation for the values between each census observation.

Figure 6 shows the average across these fourteen states for this measure. The primary difference is that rising taxation at the end of our period only keeps pace with rising economic output. Figure 7 shows property taxes as a share of output in each state.

3.1.2 Ad Valorem Property Tax Rates

We complement our main measure of property taxes levied or collected with the ad valorem rates applied each year to taxable property. In the postwar period, this measure is straightforward. The Reconstruction conventions of 1867/8 established equal and uniform property tax systems in each Southern state. The ad valorem rate, therefore, is just the annual ad valorem rate as determined by

---

[37] Unfortunately, this information is unavailable before 1840.

[38] The value of agriculture plus manufacturing output does not include the value of services. Therefore, it is not a perfect substitute for income. Unfortunately, state-based measures of nominal income are not available as frequently as agriculture and manufacturing output. We chose to use the consistently available measure.

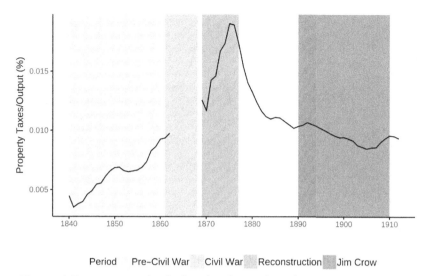

Figure 6 Property taxes/agricultural and manufacturing output, 1840–1910 three-year moving average

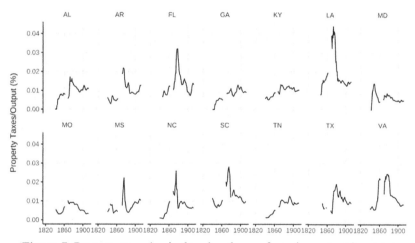

Figure 7 Property taxes/agricultural and manufacturing output by state, 1840–1910

the state government.[39] We use this annual rate for each year in the postwar period.

It is more difficult to report a consistent measure of property tax rates across each Southern state between 1820 and 1860. As mentioned, most states began

---

[39] Tax rates were typically established by a statute passed each year by the state legislature. In some instances (e.g., Georgia), the legislature set the amount it wanted to collect for specific spending items (e.g., common schools). They would then empower the governor or comptroller/auditor to set the ad valorem rate that would likely yield this amount.

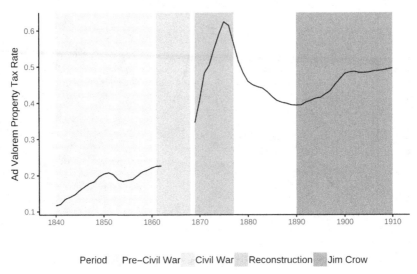

Period   Pre–Civil War   Civil War   Reconstruction   Jim Crow

Figure 8 Ad valorem property rate, 1840–1910 three-year moving average

the period setting fixed amounts to taxable property (e.g., land taxed by category, capitation taxes on slaves based on gender and age, fixed amounts for farm animals). By 1860, nine of the fourteen states had adopted systems that closely resembled the uniform property tax systems implemented during Reconstruction. We exclude states prior to their establishing uniform and universal property tax systems, so some states are not included in this measure during the prewar period. Furthermore, some changes over time in the average property tax rate during this period reflect composition effects, as states enter the data set only when they established a uniform property tax system.

Figure 8 shows the average ad valorem property tax rates across states between 1840 and 1910.[40] The pattern is strongly consistent with property taxes PWC and as a share of output as shown in Figures 4 and 6, respectively. It suggests that the increases in property taxes observed in the immediate prewar, Reconstruction, and Jim Crow periods, respectively, were due to the choice to increase property taxes; this is similarly true for the periods of declining property taxes.

3.1.3 Property Tax Incidence

The extreme wealth inequality of the South, combined with exemptions and the fact that most wealth was tied to slaves (pre-1860) and land meant that

---

[40] Due to the paucity of states with a uniform and universal property tax system at the beginning of our period, we begin our sample in 1840.

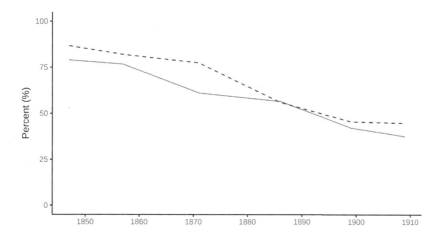

- - Agricultural Output Share —— Rural Property Tax Share

Figure 9 Agricultural output and exclusively rural share of property taxes
(%) eight-state average 1846–1910

property taxes were probably mildly to extremely progressive, with much of
the burden falling on planters (Wright 1978; Thornton 1982; Ransom 2001).
Although we lack the individual-level data necessary to confirm this supposi-
tion, we were able to decompose the property tax burden by economic sectors
and by geographic regions within states to get a sense of whether the tax burden was shifted to urban areas or to rural areas disproportionately inhabited by
poor Whites.

Figure 9 shows the proportion of total property taxes paid by the rural sector between the mid-1840s and 1910 for the eight states (Alabama, Arkansas,
Florida, Georgia, Louisiana, North Carolina, South Carolina, and Tennessee)
where we can decompose tax burdens by sector – urban, rural, or undefined –
across time.[41] The figure includes the rural tax share and a second line for the
agricultural share of total output (comprising agricultural and manufacturing
activities). Several things are worth noting. First, taxes on rural land and slaves
alone exceeded 75 percent of the prewar property tax take on average across

---

[41] Rural includes all property taxes on rural land and farm structures, farm animals (cattle, horses,
pigs), farm equipment, and, in the prewar period, the enslaved – nearly 95 percent of the
South's enslaved population resided in rural areas (Goldin 1976). Urban includes all taxes
on manufacturing assets (factories), all urban land and buildings, mining assets, merchandise,
intangible assets, and assets of businesses, such as banks and insurance companies. We omitted from either category all assets that we could not determine as fitting exclusively into either
one, including railroads, the value of individually owned money on deposits, bonds, household items, and other forms of personal property. This unspecified category also includes what
many states classified in their reports as "other property."

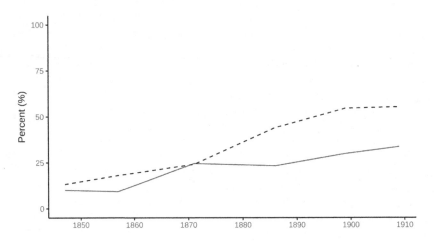

Figure 10 Manufacturing output and exclusively urban share of property
taxes (%) eight-state average, 1846–1910

the eight states. Second, while the average share of agricultural output in these
eight states falls from almost 90 percent in 1850 to less than 50 percent by
1910, the share of property taxes paid by the rural sector in these states closely
mirrors its share of output throughout the entire period. Third, the rural share of
property taxes diverges the most from the output share line when the planters
are at their least powerful politically (during Reconstruction).

Figure 10 shows the share of total property taxes falling explicitly on
urban/industrialist assets together with the manufacturing share of total output. While the share of property taxes borne by this emerging sector rises over
time, it clearly does not keep pace with the industrial share of output, particularly after rural elites regain uncontested control in the late nineteenth century.
Furthermore, the urban sector pays its highest share (and the rural sector its
lowest share) relative to the trends in output shares during Reconstruction, precisely the period in which rural elites' control was weakest. Combined, these
two figures give no indication that changes in the levels of property taxes can
be attributed to the ability of rural elites to disproportionately pass the burden
onto the emerging industrial sector.

In a separate test, we examine the distribution of state property taxes levied in
each county. We find that the association between Black population share and
these taxes is not only consistently positive and statistically significant in each
decade between 1860 and 1910, but also remarkably stable over time. The fact
that the coefficients are strongly positive (and not negative or indistinguishable
from zero) indicates that the spatial distribution of the tax burden remained

skewed toward areas with a higher Black population share, which were also the areas inhabited by relatively wealthier rural Whites.

Finally, one concern may be that enslavers used the adoption of a uniform tax system to pass the incidence of taxation onto the assets of non-rural elites. We have the property tax by sector for three states before and after they switched to a full ad valorem uniform/universal property tax system (Florida, Georgia, and Louisiana). The rural sector's share of property taxes increased from 82 percent to 92 percent in Florida, and from 69 percent to 77 percent in Georgia; in Louisiana, the share remained unchanged at exactly 79 percent.[42]

3.2 Other Measures of Taxation

As mentioned, we also collected several other measures of taxation. Specifically, we include the total amount of tax revenues collected annually into the state treasury (1820–1910), poll tax rates levied (1820–1910), and total state and local property taxes levied between 1860 and 1910. These data show us the importance of focusing on property taxes to understand the incidence of taxation in the South between 1820 and 1910. We describe each of these measures in this section.

3.2.1 Total State Tax Revenues Collected

The first measure is the total amount of tax revenues collected each year into each state treasury. In addition to property taxes, this measure often includes poll taxes, occupation and licensing taxes (i.e., a license to operate a billiards hall or sell pianos), liquor taxes, and bank, insurance, and business taxes, among others. As stated, we prefer to focus on property taxes for two interdependent reasons. For one, we are interested in the incidence of direct taxation borne primarily by the rich, which included the relatively small planter elite that dominated Southern politics. Focusing on property taxes is also appropriate because they comprised most of total state taxes in this period (roughly 74 percent of total tax revenues).[43]

3.2.2 Total State and Local Property Taxes Levied

We are, however, interested in the amount of property taxes levied by substate governments as well (i.e., counties, municipalities, and school districts). Unlike

---

[42] In the other six prewar uniform/universal ad valorem property tax states, they either switched prior to 1840 or their reports do not provide sufficient information to do this analysis.

[43] As Figure A1 shows, in each state, the correlation between total tax revenues and property taxes is extremely high (the average R-squared is 0.96).

Northern states, where local taxation was much higher than state taxes (and was rising throughout the period of our study), taxation was much more centralized in Southern states, presumably reflecting the influence the small planter elite had not only over Southern politics but also over state constitutional design (Margo 2007; Go and Lindert 2010; Chacón and Jensen 2020a). The amount of local taxation was strictly limited, and in many cases prohibited (e.g., for school purposes).

Nonetheless, the levying of local property taxes occurred in each state. Unfortunately, no Southern state provided the amount of local taxation levied, especially not in a consistent, complete, or systematic way. We therefore rely on US Census *Wealth, Debt, and Taxation* reports from 1860 to 1912 for the amount of property taxes levied at the substate level approximately once every ten years. While much less complete than our state-level data, these data can tell us whether substitution effects contribute to the observed patterns in our state-level property tax data, rather than the factors emphasized by our argument. In general, during this period, local taxes rose rapidly in the rest of the United States while state taxation either stagnated or even declined (Wallis 2000). Thus, it is plausible that our argument for why state-level property taxes declined in some periods may be capturing national trends.

As before, we normalize this measure of total property taxes levied by the White population and by agricultural and manufacturing output. The figures for each measure between 1860 and 1910 are shown in Figures 11 and 12,

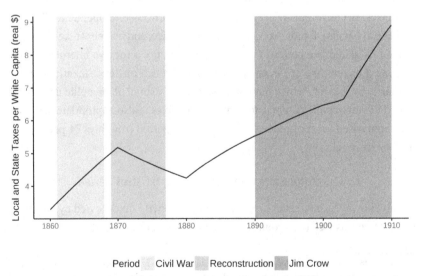

Figure 11 Local and state taxes/White population (real $, fourteen-state average), 1860–1910

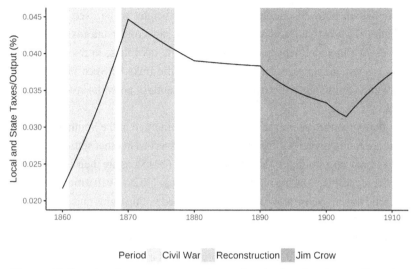

Figure 12 Local and state taxes as a share of agricultural and manufacturing output (fourteen-state average), 1860–1910

respectively. While we are unable to assess the prewar trends, postwar total state and local property taxes levied PWC and as a share of output, strongly resemble the patterns witnessed in state property taxes. Thus, despite growing urbanization and industrialization – especially in a few states with rapidly growing urban areas, such as Louisiana (New Orleans), Maryland (Baltimore), and Missouri (St. Louis, Kansas City) – it appears that the factors influencing state taxation were likely similar to those determining local property taxation.

3.2.3 Poll Tax Rates

Last, we collected the poll tax rate levied on eligible adult males in each state between 1820 and 1910, which we use as a generic proxy for taxes on lower-income groups. Poll or capitation taxes are highly regressive (as an equal tax is levied on each eligible resident regardless of means), and a few states (e.g., Maryland) constitutionally forbid them.[44] During the period under consideration, most states constitutionally required that poll tax revenues be used only on common schools in the county in which they were collected (except

---

[44] In the Southern states between 1820 and 1910, poll taxes were never levied on women or men below the age of twenty-one. Men above some age, often fifty or sixty, were also frequently exempt. While free Blacks in the prewar period often paid a rate that was much higher than the White rate (to incentivize their emigration), we only use the poll tax rate on Whites in the prewar period. In the postwar period, the same poll tax rate was levied equally on all eligible adult males.

Texas, which allowed one-third of poll tax revenues to be used for general revenue). In most states, state treasurers did not collect the tax, and in no case did we include them with property or state tax totals. In the 1890s (Jim Crow), Southern states began instituting specific links between poll tax payments and voting rights, disenfranchising thousands of potential voters, notably Blacks.[45]

Importantly, the types of tax-vote links that emerged in the South during Jim Crow are fundamentally different from those observed in other settings, such as the Prussian case studied by Mares and Queralt (2015), as are their implications for elite incentives. During the period of our study (1820–1910), most Southern states did not have electoral rules that conditioned voting rights on tax payments and, when they did, the right to vote was tied to the payment of the poll tax – which is not a property tax, and therefore not part of our dependent variable.[46] According to Mares and Queralt, the presence of a vote-tax link increases the incentives of elites to raise those taxes that condition political participation in order to disenfranchise the poor. In the US South, rural elites restricted political participation of low-income groups, targeting Blacks in particular, through a variety of mechanisms unrelated to the property tax. Furthermore, the poll tax was a trivial source of revenue.[47] In other words, our argument and evidence elucidate why agrarian elites increased taxation on themselves even when these taxes could not be used as barriers to political participation.

This measure of poll tax rates attempts to capture whether rises or declines in property taxes, which are borne primarily by a small elite, accompany changes in poll taxes, which fall most heavily on the electorate more broadly. Since the rate reflects a monetary value, we deflate this measure. States that did not levy a poll tax are coded as zero.

Figure 13 shows the average poll tax across these states from 1820 to 1910. Poll taxes on Whites are significantly lower in the prewar period. In the postwar period, when these taxes were primarily allocated to common schools, they are

---

[45] According to Kousser (1974), one of the designers of Mississippi's 1890 poll tax suffrage requirement called it the "most effective instrumentality of Negro disfranchisement."

[46] Porter (1918) shows that weak tax-vote links (e.g., when/where they existed, the rates were negligible) were somewhat common in Northern colonies/states before the Civil War. Among Southern states, antebellum North Carolina required voters to have paid some tax to be eligible to vote, but was not explicit about which tax (p. 106). A Georgia law from 1798 required all prior-year tax assessments to have been paid before voting, though enforcement may have been haphazard (pp. 125, 160).

[47] For example, in 1910, Alabama state-level property tax revenues were twelve times higher than the amount collected from poll taxes statewide.

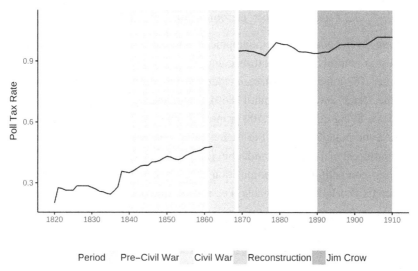

Period   Pre–Civil War   Civil War   Reconstruction   Jim Crow

Figure 13 Poll tax rate (fourteen-state average), 1820–1910 three-year moving average

higher but unchanging.[48] It is evident that changes in poll tax rates do not follow the patterns exhibited by property taxes, ad valorem property tax rates, or total tax revenues.

3.3 Other Data

We briefly describe other data used to assess our argument.

3.3.1 Public Spending and Collective Goods

Our argument states that elites will support increasing property taxation if they have political control *and* valuable collective goods exist that can further their economic interests. Thus, any test of our argument must include evidence on the *types* of spending in which the state was engaged. While not as complete as our taxation data, we include two measures of collective goods that elites clearly valued in particular periods of our study. For the prewar period, we examine public spending on railroads. In the post-Reconstruction period, we use an original data set of state public spending on colleges and universities between 1880 and 1910. We contrast this with public spending on a redistributive good that should be more coveted by poorer residents: state spending on common schools. We describe each of these measures in more detail in what follows.

---

[48] Most of the observed changes reflect the effects of deflating this measure rather than changes in nominal rates.

3.3.2 Demographic, Economic, and Political Variables

We use several additional demographic, economic, and political variables primarily as controls. Most controls come from the various decennial censuses between 1820 and 1910. These include once-a-decade values for population (White, Black, and enslaved until 1860), the urbanization rate (share of a state's residents living in cities of 2,500 or more people), and economic output (agriculture and manufacturing). For each measure, we use linear interpolation for the non-decennial years. From Dubin (2007), we created several measures of partisan competition and composition of each state's legislature over time. Appendix B details each variable (i.e., sources and operationalization).

4 Property Taxes before the Civil War

We first test our argument about the importance of political control for elites and their demand for collective goods in the prewar period. We exploit the presence of a lasting international commodity price shock, which increased the value of production and therefore the demand for capital-intensive infrastructure by slaveholding elites. The key to increasing production was constructing a railroad network that would allow for the cultivation of lands that were too far from navigable water to profitably use enslaved labor. This would require extensive increases in public revenues to finance such a network in the vast and sparsely populated South. We contend that elites will support increasing taxation only if they control spending *and* this control of political power is likely to persist. We argue that variation across states in state legislative apportionment rules – which gave disproportionate influence to large slaveholders in the legislatures of some states but not others – meant that elites in the malapportioned states enjoyed greater political control and would therefore have stronger incentives to support increasing taxation.

Indeed, we show that: 1) the rise in property tax revenues PWC and as a share of output, respectively, were substantially higher in states where legislative malapportionment provided the plantation class with a firmer grip on enduring political power; 2) property tax rates in the malapportioned states (MS) rose faster than those in the non-malapportioned states (NMS); 3) regressive poll taxes, which were levied more broadly across the White population, did not increase faster in the MS; and 4) increased revenue was allocated toward collective goods that furthered the economic interests of slaveholders (railroads) and not toward goods (public education) that would benefit the White population more generally.[49]

---

[49] This evidence builds on previous work, which uses this same international price-shock strategy to show that *total* state tax revenues, rather than property taxes, rose more in the MS between 1844 and 1860 (Jensen, Pardelli, and Timmons 2023).

4.1 Property Taxes between 1820 and 1860

Our period begins in the 1820s, at which point there were eleven Southern states. As chattel slavery moved westward into the Southwest Territory (area won in the 1783 Treaty of Paris from the UK) and the newly acquired Louisiana Purchase (area acquired from France in 1803), the original five coastal British colonies were joined as states by Kentucky (1792), Tennessee (1796), Louisiana (1812), Mississippi (1816), Alabama (1819), and Missouri (1821). As shown in Figure 4, property taxes PWC collected in the 1820s were low compared to any time after 1845. Beyond some critical functions, such as courts and the enforcement of enslaved property rights (i.e., regulation of slave patrols and the state militia), the infrastructural capacity of these states was minimal and the governments did relatively little. There was very little systematic funding for public education or infrastructure such as canals and turnpikes.[50]

Yet, even at this low level of public spending, property taxes on average would decline even further in the 1830s. In an economic boom spurred on by substantial land speculation and a commodity bubble, state governments found alternative nontax sources of revenue. In particular, states successfully used their monopoly power on the incorporation of banks to generate rent profits that poured into the state treasury as dividends (Wallis 2005). In addition to revenues gained from taxes on and dividends from state banks, substantial additional revenues came from land sales, loans, and even briefly the surplus revenue paid out by the federal government in 1836. These temporary windfalls even led some states, such as Alabama, Georgia, and Maryland, to eliminate property taxes altogether. The loans taken on by Southern states in particular financed so-called land banks, used primarily by enslavers to finance the speculative boom in land and slaves of this period (Wallis 2005).

The Panic of 1837 ushered in roughly seven years of deflationary and economically depressed conditions. The long-lasting downturn caused debt defaults across the economy, including on the state debt of four Southern states (Arkansas, Louisiana, Maryland, and Mississippi), as well as the territory of Florida. Sources of nontax revenue evaporated and states needed to raise tax revenues to finance their debts and fund government operations.

While the increase in property taxes between the mid-1840s and the onset of the Civil War that is apparent in Figures 4 and 6 may capture some of the need to finance debts, this period also coincided with a substantial increase

---

[50] Southern fiscal inactivity during the 1820s was in stark contrast to the large and expensive publicly financed infrastructure projects undertaken in a number of Northern states, such as New York, Ohio, and Pennsylvania (Larson 2002). Maryland was a clear exception among Southern states, as was Virginia to a much lesser extent.

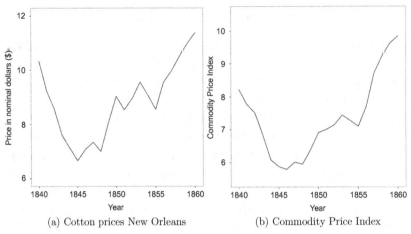

(a) Cotton prices New Orleans   (b) Commodity Price Index

Figure 14 Cotton prices ($) and Commodity Price Index, 1840–1860
(five-year moving average)

across Southern states in public spending on railroads (Heath 1950; Fishlow 1965; Goodrich 1974). In turn, this period witnessed a sustained boom in the international demand for Southern cash crops that relied on enslaved labor, notably cotton. In both New Orleans and Liverpool, the primary international market for cotton, the price of "Middling American cotton" and sugar more than doubled between the mid-1840s and late 1850s. Tobacco prices in Liverpool rose more than threefold between 1843 and 1857 (Gray and Thompson 1933, p. 492, 1026, 1033–1038). Figure 14 shows how the rising demand for Southern export crops affected commodity prices between 1840 and 1860. Specifically, Figure 14 (a) shows the five-year moving average of cotton prices in New Orleans from 1840 and 1860; Figure 14 (b) shows the five-year moving average of a commodity index reflecting variation in cotton, sugar, and tobacco prices over the same period.

These price increases coincided with a production boom in these crops. Southern cotton production exceeded 2.2 billion pounds in 1860, up from less than 800 million in 1840. Sugar production also nearly tripled over this period (Gray and Thompson 1933, p. 1033), while tobacco exports rose almost fivefold (Gray and Thompson 1933, pp. 1033–1036).

Surging international prices and rapidly rising production enriched the relatively small group of Southern enslavers. For instance, the value of cotton exports rose from approximately $50,000,000 in 1846 to nearly $200,000,000 by 1860 (North 1960, p. 233).[51] As stated by Ransom (2001), "There could

---

[51] Approximately 75 percent of cotton produced was exported; cotton exports alone comprised more than half of the total value of American exports in this period.

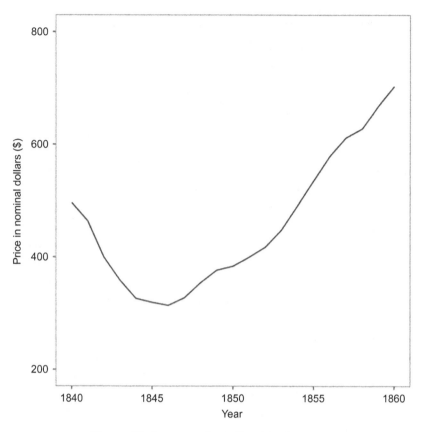

Figure 15 Average prices of enslaved persons

be little doubt that the prosperity of the slave economy rested on its ability to produce cotton more efficiently than any other region of the world." In turn, international demand for cash crops and the increased ability of Southern enslavers to meet this demand strongly influenced the value of their enslaved property. To wit, the late 1830s and 1840s depression in cotton prices was followed by declines in the average value of slaves, as captured by prices of major Southern slave auctions. As shown in Figure 15, the surge in international prices for cash crops was similarly followed by rapid increases in the value of slaves.

While the desire to meet rising international demand for these cash crops was clearly in enslavers' economic interest, the limitations of the existing infrastructure network severely constrained their ability to do so. Millions of acres of otherwise fertile land went uncultivated due to their distance from navigable waters, rendering the use of expensive enslaved labor unprofitable. As was the case for non-slaveholders across the United States, substantial investments in infrastructure, such as canals and railroads, were necessary to connect vast amounts of potential farmland to markets. Furthermore, the lack of investment in infrastructure was an important source for Southern underdevelopment compared to the North (Wright 2022).

One option for enslavers would be to finance the construction of railroads privately, as was the case in the UK and many of the Northern states. As we argued earlier, increasing the fiscal capacity of the states, as would be required to finance large-scale railroad construction, would be risky if the state government came to be controlled by the non-slaveholding majority. Yet privately financing the construction of railroad network on the scale required to unlock millions of remote and uncultivated potential farmland was completely infeasible: the costs and risks to private capital were far too high, and expectations of satisfactory returns were unlikely to be fulfilled in the sparsely populated and capital-poor South (Heath 1950; Fishlow 1965; Goodrich 1974; Larson 2002).[52] According to Reed (1962, p. 184), for example, "seventy-five per cent of the railroads chartered in the 1830s [in Louisiana] failed to materialize [due to constraints on capital]." More broadly, Larson (2002, p. 239) claimed that the South was too "underdeveloped and incapable of supporting large-scale internal improvements on the strength of private fortunes alone." The federal government was also not a viable solution; instead, public financing of infrastructure would need to come from Southern state and local governments (Wallis and Weingast 2018). Unlike in the North, the South's lack of large urban areas also meant that Southern state governments would need to be the primary source for public funding (Fishlow 1965, p. 397). As Marrs (2009, p. 24) argues: "States proved to be a critical solution to the problem of railroad financing in the South." Changes in infrastructure technology and international commodity markets meant that the economic interests of enslavers would be furthered by raising taxation on themselves to finance railroad construction. These large investments in public infrastructure financed by self-taxation would not only open up more land for cultivation but would also increase the demand for and the value of slaves, the primary asset of enslavers.

4.2 Variation in De Jure Political Control

We argue that Southern states in which enslavers had greater political control were more likely to respond to this rising demand for these crops by increasing property taxes on themselves in order to fund railroad construction that would further their economic interests. We exploit the fact that in seven of the fourteen

---

[52] While the Northern states were more capital-poor than the UK, they had much deeper capital markets and were much more densely populated than states in the South.

states, representation in both chambers of the state legislature was systemati- cally malapportioned in favor of higher slave-share districts (e.g., counties); representation in both chambers of the other seven Southern states was based on the principle of "one [adult White] man, one vote." In the seven MS, the bias was due to: 1) representation based on total population including the enslaved, or capped representation that limited urban areas (e.g., Baltimore, New Orle- ans), 2) using the amount of taxes paid as the basis (which favored highly enslaved areas), or 3) the use of a fixed basis of representation, regardless of dif- ferences and changes in population. In the NMS, legislative representation was determined by each county's White or eligible voter population, and required frequent reapportionment to capture spatial shifts in population.[53] The states that comprise the MS and the NMS are reported in Table 2. For each state, the table also shows the basis of representation in the legislature.

Legislative malapportionment provided a source of political power to enslavers. The economic geography of slavery meant that enslavers were typically spatially concentrated within each state.[54] Thus, systems of appor- tionment that overrepresented highly slave-dependent areas – whether by including slaves in the population count, basing representation on taxes paid, or using a fixed basis that overrepresented less populated rural areas[55] – could, despite their minority status, manufacture majorities for enslavers in the state legislatures.

The political power malapportionment provided was also enduring. This de jure electoral rule was "self-enforcing." Because apportionment rules were enshrined in each state's constitutions, the slaveholding elite need not expend resources to maintain them.[56] Furthermore, legislative majorities conferred by malapportionment allowed enslavers to block any equalizing reforms they opposed. Given this effective veto, it is unsurprising that none of the seven MS reformed their apportionment rules to a White-population basis. Legislative dominance was also critical in this period, as the other branches (the executive, the judiciary) were weak. Simply put, control of the state legislature meant control of the state government (Green 1966; Thornton 2014). In sum, malap- portionment increased both the current power of enslavers and their expectation of future control.

---

[53] By the 1850s, almost all adult White males were eligible to vote (Keyssar 2001).

[54] Figure A2 shows the geographic distribution of slavery across the South.

[55] Less than 4 percent of the enslaved resided in the South's urban counties (1860 Census).

[56] An analogous example is that low-population American states do not need to expend resources to maintain the enormous advantages in the US Senate conferred by the two-senators-per-state mandate of the US Constitution.

Table 2 Slave states and state legislative representation

	Basis of representation	
	Upper house (Senate) (1)	Lower house (H. of Rep.) (2)
Malapportioned States (MS)		
Florida	federal pop.	federal pop.
Georgia	fixed (1)	federal pop.*
Louisiana	total pop.*	total pop.*
Maryland	fixed (1)	total pop.*
North Carolina	taxation	federal pop.
South Carolina	fixed (1)	taxation
Virginia	fixed	fixed
Non-malapportioned States (NMS)		
Alabama	White pop.	White pop.
Arkansas	White males	White males
Kentucky	qualified voters	qualified voters
Mississippi	White pop.	White pop.
Missouri	White pop.	White pop.
Tennessee	qualified voters	qualified voters
Texas	free pop.	free pop.

Note: Federal population refers to the formula by which enslaved persons were counted as three-fifths of a person for the purposes of apportionment (as was the case with the US Constitution until the Fourteenth Amendment [1868]). An asterisk indicates states in which a maximum number of representatives/senators could be apportioned to any individual district. The number in parentheses denotes states in which each administrative district received an equal number of representatives/senators.

Using malapportionment status to test our argument may lead to omitted variable bias if its adoption is not exogenous to the factors influencing taxation and spending on railroads. In each of the seven MS, this bias to legislative representation can be traced to the colonial era. Higher enslaved-share areas were overrepresented in colonial legislatures (Beramendi and Jensen 2019), which was carried over into the initial postindependence constitutions (Green 1966, pp. 97–98).[57] Simply put, disproportionate enslaver power was locked in

---

[57] Appendix C outlines the origins of each state's system of apportionment. It also provides evidence that differences across states in this legislative feature are unrelated to the factors that

long before the advent of railroads, as well as before the invention of the cotton gin and commercialization of cotton – Florida (1846) being the one exception. In the seven NMS, a population basis of apportionment was adopted in their initial constitutions and persisted throughout the antebellum period. The critical factor determining whether a new state adopted a biased basis of apportionment was whether the slaveholding elite was well established before statehood and able to implement this bias in the pre-statehood legislature (whether colonial or territorial).

This is not to say that enslavers in the NMS did not also possess disproportionate political power (e.g., Wooster 1969; Thornton 2014). Rather, the consequence for enslavers in the NMS was that power was always more contestable. These elites had to consider whether the upside of more collective goods in the present period was worth the potential costs of political power in their now fiscally enhanced state being in the hands of the non-slaveholding majority.

Figure 16 shows the fourteen states by their malapportionment status and the share of their total population who were enslaved in 1860. While the average enslaved share in the MS (38 percent) exceeded that of the NMS (30 percent), there was great variation across both institutional groupings. Of the six states

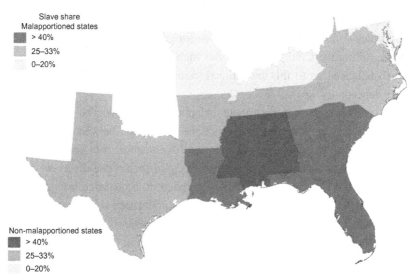

Figure 16 Apportionment status and enslaved share (% of pop.), 1860

---

caused divergence in prewar property taxes and public support for railroads, and uses original data on representation to demonstrate the persistence and magnitude of this bias in favor of enslavers in the MS, and the lack of bias in favor of enslavers in the NMS.

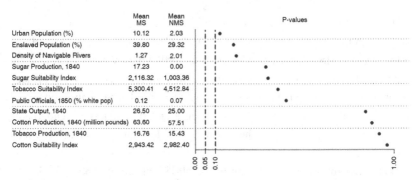

Figure 17 Balance test for pretreatment covariates, 1840
Note: Differences between (MS) and (NMS). Cotton, sugar, and tobacco suitability indices reflect the maximum potential yield based on climate, soil, and growing conditions as estimated by the UN Food and Agriculture Organization (FAO). Shares of urban and enslaved population; cotton, sugar, and tobacco production; and state output are measured in 1840. Density of navigable rivers (representing the total length of rivers over the surface area of each state) is obtained from Atack (2015); and the share of public officials PWC is measured in 1850 (no prior census provides this information). See Table B4 for more details on sources.

in which the enslaved share was greater than 40 percent – the so-called cotton states – two, Alabama and Mississippi, were non-malapportioned. In the five states whose enslaved share ranged between 20 percent and 40 percent of the total population, three were non-malapportioned. Of the three remaining "border" states – those with less than 20 percent enslaved share and who did not secede during the Civil War – one was malapportioned. Thus, the states are mostly balanced across this institutional feature at three very different levels of slave dependency.

To further mitigate concerns about malapportionment status being correlated with other factors that could influence the association between commodity prices and taxation outcomes, in Figure 17 we conduct a balance test over a number of state-level characteristics that could predict the divergent fiscal trajectories we observe. The variables included in the balance test are: total population, enslaved population share, urban population share, state output, number of state officials PWC, and density of navigable rivers, as well as measures of agricultural suitability and production of cotton, sugar, and tobacco.[58] A statistically significant correlation between apportionment status and one of these covariates would suggest the presence of a potential alternative explanation for the decision of states to increase taxation. Different levels of cotton suitability between the MS and NMS, for example, would indicate that one

---

[58] See Table B4 for sources and additional details on each variable.

group had more to gain from increasing taxation and investing in railroads than the other. Similarly, divergent cotton production levels in 1840 would suggest that some states benefited from greater productive capabilities when commodity prices began to rise. Differences in the initial stock of bureaucratic capacity may have allowed some states to raise taxes more rapidly than others, or created uneven incentives to invest in fiscal capacity (Lee and Paine 2022). Finally, the density of navigable rivers also matters in that it may have made the need for railroads more pressing in some areas than in others. We find no statistically significant differences in any of these covariates across MS and NMS.

In short, circa 1840, our comparison states had roughly similar endowments. They differed primarily on the supply side: in half of the states, the slaveholding elite's power to control taxes and public spending was substantially less contested in both the present period and for the foreseeable future; in the other half, their control was less certain. Whereas the commodity boom increased the value of land and slaves, and infrastructure bottlenecks constrained those assets from reaching their full potential across both the MS and NMS, only the elite in the MS had the power and incentive to use their secure hold on power to tax themselves to finance collective goods that would leverage the boom for their benefit. We thus expect tax and spending differentials to emerge across the two types of states, with the MS increasing the incidence of taxation on their elites and public spending on railroads at a faster clip than their NMS counterparts.

4.3 Results

We begin with visual evidence that rising commodity prices translated into a greater rise in property taxes in the MS compared to the NMS. Figures 18 and 19 show the trend in the average property taxes PWC (1820–60) and as a share of output (1840–60), respectively. Although both follow largely similar trajectories until the early 1840s, they quickly and noticeably diverge when commodity prices begin to increase, as predicted. Since these differences could, in theory, be driven by distinct levels of state capacity or uneven patterns of economic growth, in Figure 20 we examine the trends in ad valorem property tax rates over the same period.[59]

To evaluate whether changes in commodity prices disproportionately affect property taxes in the MS during this period, our empirical strategy adopts the following difference-in-differences approach:[60]

$$y_{it} = \beta_0 lnC_t + \beta_1 lnC_t \times M_{it} + \beta_2 \mathbf{X}_{it} + \lambda_i + \gamma_t + \epsilon_{it}, \tag{1}$$

---

[59] Unfortunately, the rate measure is not consistently available for all states throughout the period under analysis. As a result, some of the observed variation may reflect missing data.

[60] See, e.g., Dube and Vargas (2013); Garfias (2018).

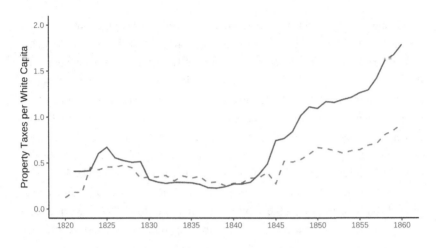

States − · Non-malapportioned — Malapportioned

Figure 18 Property taxes/White population (real $), 1820–1860
Malapportioned versus non-malapportioned states

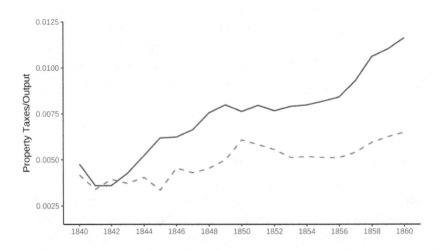

States − · Non-malapportioned — Malapportioned

Figure 19 Property taxes/agricultural and manufacturing output, 1840–1860
Malapportioned versus non-malapportioned states

where y_{it} is a state-level measure of property tax revenues or ad valorem rates, for state i at time t. M_{it} is an indicator variable that takes the value 1 if the state legislature of state i is malapportioned in year t, and 0 otherwise. Our main variable of interest C_t reflects cotton prices (logged) in year t. The parameter β_1 captures the differential effect of commodity prices on property taxes in

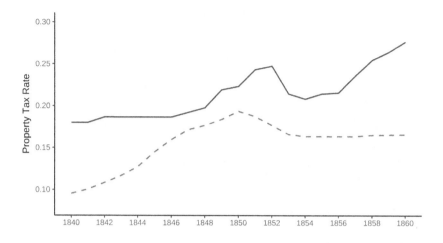

States − · Non-malapportioned — Malapportioned

Figure 20 Property tax rates, 1840–1860 Malapportioned versus
non-malapportioned states

the MS. Both dependent and independent variables are measured as three-year
moving averages to reduce small fluctuations. X_{it} represents a vector of time-
varying covariates; λ_i and γ_t are respectively state and year fixed effects, and
ϵ_{it} is an error term.

Table 3 shows our benchmark models investigating the effect of apportionment status and commodity prices on total state property taxation PWC without
any additional covariates. The second column includes time-varying controls,
namely total population (log), urban population (log), and total output (log).
The third column includes the same covariates, but measured in 1840, to minimize potential concerns about posttreatment bias, and interacted with year
indicators. The estimates are substantively similar across specifications. The
positive and significant interaction term between apportionment status and cotton prices captures the predicted moderation effect. As expected, an increase
in international commodity prices differentially affects tax revenues in the MS,
where elites have full control of the state apparatus.[61] To address the concern
that cotton prices might be endogenous, in Appendix Table A1, we adopt an

---

[61] A key assumption required to interpret these results causally is that, in the absence of an
increase in commodity prices, taxation outcomes in the MS and NMS would have followed
a similar trajectory. Although untestable, this assumption implies that fiscal trends in these
two groups of states should be parallel prior to the price shock. Appendix Figures A3 and A4
show that this is the case for both state property taxes as a share of output and PWC. In both
figures, the trajectories of property taxes in the MS and NMS are almost identical prior to the
rise in commodity prices. Over time, we observe a meaningful divergence between these two
groups, with the MS experiencing larger increases in taxation.

Table 3 Antebellum period: Property taxes, cotton prices, and malapportionment status

	Dependent variable		
	Property taxes per White capita (real $)		
	(1)	(2)	(3)
Cotton prices ×	2.057***	1.959***	2.087***
Malapportionment	(0.631)	(0.565)	(0.605)
State fixed effects	Yes	Yes	Yes
Year fixed effects	Yes	Yes	Yes
Geographic controls	Yes	Yes	Yes
Time-varying covariates	No	Yes	No
Time-invariant covariates	No	No	Yes
Observations	268	268	259
R^2	0.429	0.476	0.623

Note: Main variables measured as three-year moving averages. Geographic controls are: state area, cotton suitability, and river density. These covariates are interacted with year indicators. Time-varying covariates are: state population (log), urban population share, and log of total output (agriculture and manufacturing). Column 1 includes geographic controls only; column 2 includes geographic controls and time-varying covariates. Column 3 includes the same covariates measured in 1840 (pretreatment) interacted with year indicators. $*p<0.1$; $**p<0.05$; $***p<0.01$.

alternative measure for our independent variable, a commodity price index weighted by the relative suitability of each state to the cultivation of three main crops: cotton, sugar, and tobacco. This measure reflects the exposure of states to fluctuations in international commodity prices at any given point in time based on their suitability to the cultivation of each crop relative to the Southern average. We also evaluate the possibility that coastal status and access to the Mississippi River might correlate with malapportionment and explain our results (see Table A2). Our substantive results remain unchanged.

Figure 21 shows that poll tax rates do not follow the same pattern: there is no difference in either levels or trends across the two groups of states. In fact, this figure indicates that unlike property taxes, regressive poll taxes did not rise in the MS. Consistent with Thornton's (1982) assessment that the wealthiest third of the citizenry paid at least two-thirds of all taxes during the antebellum period, these results suggest that elites in the MS financed state-level fiscal expansion by taxing themselves, eschewing taxes that fell more heavily on the non-slaveholding White majority.

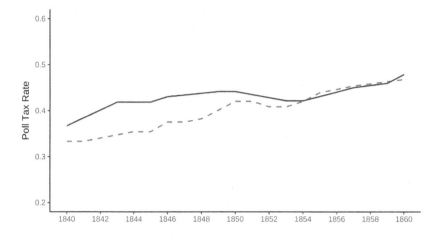

States − ·Non-malapportioned— Malapportioned

Figure 21 Poll tax rates, 1840–1860 Malapportioned versus
non-malapportioned states

4.4 Collective Goods for Elites: Railroads versus Education

A critical aspect of our argument is that economic elites will support increasing taxation on themselves if this revenue funds collective goods that enhance their interests. We now turn to railroad construction and trends in public education; the former disproportionately favored elites, while the latter, presumably, disproportionately benefited the average White citizen.[62]

To measure public support for railroads, we rely on data presented by Heath (1950), who collected all public (federal, state, and local) spending on railroads in the South prior to 1861. In total, at least $144 million of public funds were spent constructing railroads in these states prior to 1861 (out of $252 million total [public and private] spending on railroads in the South [Fishlow 1965, p. 397]).[63] Of the public total, 57 percent of this came from state governments.[64]

---

[62] Public education was the most significant early redistributionist program in the United States and a critical pillar of future American prosperity (Goldin and Katz 2009).

[63] According to Heath (1950, p. 43), the public total is a lower bound, as it excludes many forms of public sector support (e.g., tax exemptions). At the same time, the private sector fraction is an upper bound, as companies often significantly overstated actual paid-in capital.

[64] The rest came from local governments (38 percent) and the federal government (5 percent). While substate spending was important in a few states (notably Kentucky), all states with above-average railroad mileage in 1860 had a majority of public spending on railroads come from state governments; as shown in Table 4, the three states most reliant on county and municipal expenditures (Kentucky, Louisiana, and Alabama) all had below-average railroad mileage

Table 4 Collective goods: State support for railroads, 1860

	State Government Railroad Spending			Railway Mileage	
	Railroad spending PWC	Railroad spending sh. income	State sh. public RR spending	Railway mileage PWC	Railway mileage sh. income
	($)	(%)	(%)		(%)
	(1)	(2)	(3)	(4)	(5)
Malapportioned					
Florida	62.7	39.0	89.4	0.52	0.003
Georgia	11.7	7.8	53.9	0.24	0.002
Louisiana	9.5	3.7	38.7	0.09	0.004
Maryland				0.07	0.006
North Carolina	16.9	13.6	89.3	0.14	0.001
South Carolina	33.2	17.2	70.6	0.34	0.002
Virginia	22.7	18.6	75.0	0.17	0.002
AVERAGE	30.6	16.7	72.0	0.22	0.003
Non-malapportioned					
Alabama	4.1	3.0	36.6	0.14	0.001
Arkansas	0.6	0.4	47.4	0.02	0.000
Kentucky	0.8	0.8	4.5	0.06	0.001
Mississippi	6.0	2.1	50.8	0.25	0.001
Missouri	6.6	6.6		0.08	0.001
Tennessee	20.9	20.7	66.9	0.14	0.001
Texas	0.0	0.0	0.0	0.07	0.001
AVERAGE	5.9	5.0	34.3	0.11	0.001

Note: Railroad spending comes from Heath (1950). Railway mileage was obtained from Atack (2015). PWC indicates per White capita.

We create three measures of state public spending on railroads, presented in Table 4. Column 1 shows total spending on railroads by state governments in this period as a proportion of each state's White population in 1860. On average, state government spending on railroads is approximately six times higher PWC in the MS. Column 2 normalizes state spending on railroads by state

by 1860. By comparison, in the Northern states, antebellum-era railroad spending was much more likely to come from private and local government sources (Goodrich 1974, pp. 270–271).

income in 1860. Even when normalized by income, MS governments spent three times more. Column 3 reports the share of public spending on railroads that comes from state sources. In the states in which enslavers had much greater control of state governments we see a much higher proportion of public spending occurring at the state level. Columns 4 and 5 provide railroad mileage data from Atack (2015), allowing us to assess the possibility that public spending on railroads merely cloaks rent-seeking corruption by elites in the MS. Whether normalizing total railroad mileage by White population (column 4) or state income (column 5), the MS created significantly more railway mileage on average, indicating that public funds translated into output and did not solely line the pockets of governing elites.

One concern is that we might be simply capturing demand side variation (e.g., Lee and Paine 2022) – rather than, as we argue, political supply. Our evidence suggests this is unlikely. First, as our balance and robustness tests illustrate, we fail to confirm that the geography of the NMS meant they needed fewer railroads. Second, a large historical literature has shown that strong demand for railroads existed across the South (e.g., Heath 1950; Goodrich 1974; Larson 2002). The problem of political supply rather than demand is demonstrated, for example, by Thornton (2014, p. 107), who notes the difficulty of receiving public financing in highly enslaved, but not malapportioned, Alabama: "Time and again, when a small loan or expenditure could have added millions of dollars to the commerce of the state by facilitating trade, the legislature refused to act." Third, we look at railroad miles by state in 1880, roughly ten years after Congress completely altered the political system of Southern states with Reconstruction. As evidence that state-specific demand-side factors cannot explain the large differences in prewar railroad supply, we observe no meaningful difference on average across MS and NMS in railroad mileage as a share of income (0.0029 vs. 0.0025, $p = 0.58$) and mileage PWC (0.23 vs 0.19, $p = 0.36$) in 1880.

Public Education Spending

We now turn to public education, a redistributive good that would have been much more favored by the wider electorate. The 1860 Census provides several measures of state-level support for public education, such as the sources of public financing for public *and* private schools, and White school attendance in public and private schools. We normalize this information with the White school-aged population (ages five to fourteen) and state income to create measures of enrollment rates and expenditures. Table 5 reports average spending and enrollment figures for MS (column 1) and NMS (column 2).

Table 5 State support for redistribution: Public education, 1860

	Malapportioned States (average) (1)	Non-malapportioned States (average) (2)
Panel A: School Attendance		
Whites attending school / Whites, 5–14 (%)	56.4	63.4
White public school pupils / Whites, 5–14 (%)	32.4	43.6
White public school pupils / Total pupils (%)	74.8	85.8
Panel B: State Government Spending		
State public school spending / Whites, 5–14 ($)	0.72	0.89
State public school spending / public school pupils ($)	2.12	2.06
State total educ. spending / public school and private pupils ($)	3.39	2.4

Note: All variables were constructed from the 1860 US Census. Each value is the average across the states in the MS (column 1) and NMS (column 2).

Panel A focuses on white school attendance, especially in public schools. As is evident, a greater share of White school-aged children attended school in the NMS (63 percent) than in the MS (56 percent). The census also asked state superintendents to report the number of pupils in public and private schools, respectively.[65] We thus construct two measures of state reliance on public schools: White public school pupils as a share of each state's White school-aged population and the share of total pupils (private and public school) in public schools. With both measures, the average is higher in the NMS.

Panel B focuses on state government education spending for both public and private schools. First, we compare state government spending on public schools as a share of the state's White population, ages five to fourteen. On average, it is slightly higher in the NMS (eighty-nine cents per school-aged White person versus seventy-two cents). Next, we calculate state government support as a

---

[65] In some states, the number of pupils reported by state superintendents was smaller than school attendance rates reported by households.

proportion of public school pupils. Although the MS had a greater share of students in private schools, state government spending per public school pupil was almost identical ($2.12 in the average MS versus $2.06 in NMS). The census data also allow us to construct measures of total public spending per public and private school pupil. Despite private school enrollment comprising only roughly 25 percent of total pupils in the MS, private schools received on average roughly 40 percent of state education funding. In other words, despite significantly higher taxes, the average MS did not provide more support for public education; instead, they funneled more public money toward private education. In sum, none of these measures show differences across the MS and NMS in public education supply that are remotely comparable to the gaps observed in public support for railroads.

4.5 Robustness

In the Appendix, we evaluate the robustness of our results. To minimize concerns that property taxes may be rising mechanically due to differential changes in the intensity of slavery across states, Appendix Table A3 includes the size of the enslaved population as an additional covariate in our baseline specifications. Our coefficients of interest remain largely unchanged while the size of the enslaved population has a negative (albeit not always significant) association with property taxes.[66] In Appendix C, we discuss endogeneity concerns with malapportionment, and we consider whether omitted factors may explain both malapportionment and the observed increase in property taxes in the late antebellum period. Similarly, in Appendix D, we address concerns that initial differences in state capacity may have been responsible for the uneven increase in taxation across states. We also use county-level collection of state taxes to demonstrate that greater taxes did indeed fall on the counties with higher shares of enslaved population.

5 Postwar Taxation

5.1 Reconstruction and Its Aftermath

5.1.1 Context

In the aftermath of the North's victory in the American Civil War and the Thirteenth Amendment's emancipation of nearly 4 million enslaved Americans, congressional Republicans sought to permanently weaken Southern rural

---

[66] This result is consistent with Wright's (2022) argument that because enslaved people are a mobile form of property, their value does not appreciate with local investments the way land does. In this sense, all else equal, the intensity of slavery should decrease local tax revenues and infrastructure spending.

elites' stranglehold on political power with the passage of the Military Reconstruction Acts of 1867 and 1868 (Foner 2014).[67] These acts, as a condition for regaining their seats in Congress, required ten former Confederate states to create new state constitutions granting universal adult male suffrage and to ratify the Fourteenth Amendment, which enshrined the principle of civil rights and equal protection under the law for all citizens.[68] Perhaps just as important, these acts also required the army to register adult Black males to vote and to protect their ability to exercise the franchise and run for office.

These reforms resulted in a temporary transformation of the party system, and the distribution of political power more broadly, in these ten Southern states. Immediately following the adoption of new state constitutions, which extended the franchise to all adult males, the Republican Party, which was nonexistent in the prewar South, won nine gubernatorial elections and majorities in seventeen legislative chambers (Dubin 2007, 2010). The Republican Party's initial success was driven by Black voters, who formed the backbone of the party in the South. The effectiveness of these reforms was demonstrated by the election of thousands of Black politicians and officials to local, state, and federal office throughout the South in the decade following passage of the Military Reconstruction Acts (Foner 1993).

This political revolution resulted in a substantially expanded role for the Southern states in providing redistributive public goods. According to Foner (2014, p. 364), "Serving an expanded citizenry and embracing a new definition of public responsibility, Republican government affected virtually every facet of Southern life ... Public schools, hospitals, penitentiaries, and asylums for orphans and the insane were established for the first time or received increased funding." Most dramatically, Republicans fundamentally altered the role of the state with regards to providing a public education for all children (Foner 2014, p. 366). This new redistributive spending was financed primarily by increasing property taxes on the landed elite (see Figures 4 and 6).[69]

Rising property taxes thus became an effective rallying cry for opponents of Reconstruction. Democratic leaders in many states soon organized taxpayers' conventions, where participants expressed their objection not only to the

---

[67] Republicans used their enormous congressional majorities to overcome fierce resistance from Southern Whites and Northern Democrats, as well as vetoes of each bill by President Andrew Johnson.

[68] See Table 1, column 6 for these states.

[69] Levies were so high that, according to Foner (2014, p. 376), "immense tracts fell into the hands of state governments for nonpayment of taxes – in Mississippi alone over 6 million acres, one fifth of the entire area of the state, was forfeited in this way. Stephen Duncan, the antebellum South's largest cotton producer, saw seven of his Louisiana plantations seized and sold for back taxes in 1874."

claimed profligacy of Reconstruction government but to the new purposes of public spending, such as the financing of common schools. Convinced that the increasing tax burden resulted from the fact that "nine-tenths of the members of the Legislature own no property and pay no taxes" (Foner 2014, p. 416), Democrats called for a return to rule by property holders, which entailed denying Blacks, as well as many Whites, any role in government.

The powerful backlash in response to radical changes in government was not confined to taxpayers' conventions. It also took the form of political violence, the intensity of which can scarcely be dissociated from fiscal policy: as shown by Logan (2019), Black officeholders in locations with higher taxes were more likely to be victims of attacks. In addition to the use of the US Army to suppress this violent counterrevolutionary reaction, Congress responded by passing the three Enforcement Acts empowering the newly created Department of Justice to regulate state and local elections, enforce political and civil rights, and prosecute those who impeded political participation. Through its expanded authority, the federal government was able to successfully prosecute more than 1,000 violations between 1871 and 1874, and to temporarily constrain non-state violent groups such as the Ku Klux Klan (Walton et al. 2012).

While Radical Reconstruction was briefly successful at overturning the existing political structure in these states, little was done to remedy the vastly unequal ownership of economic assets, in particular land. Despite much debate, no program of land redistribution was adopted. As a result, landownership remained highly concentrated, especially in the former plantation counties where most of the Black population lived. We argue that the persistence of this massive inequality in economic resources meant that the ability of Blacks to successfully use their newly granted political rights to influence social and economic policies required constant federal intervention on their behalf. But the federal intervention, especially in terms of the military occupation, was spatially uneven and declining in scope over time.[70]

There was also significant spatial and temporal variation in the extent to which Reconstruction was successful, as measured by the victories of the Republican Party. This variation leads to our main prediction regarding the incidence of property taxes during Reconstruction and its immediate aftermath. In five Reconstruction states – Arkansas, Florida, Louisiana, Mississippi, and South Carolina – the Republican Party was able to win unified control

---

[70] While the presence of troops has been shown to positively affect the election of Black politicians (Chacón et al. 2021) and the amount of property taxes levied (Chacón and Jensen 2020b), the size of the occupation was simply too small, not to mention declining throughout Reconstruction, to protect Black voters and politicians across the vast rural South.

of the state government (legislature and governor's office) for multiple electoral cycles in a row. South Carolina, for instance, even had a majority-Black state legislature from 1868 until 1876. We call these five Reconstruction states *Republican Control* states. We argue that this control demonstrates that federal intervention, even if only briefly, limited the ability of Southern elites to use their de facto power to overcome majoritarian preferences when de jure political rights are effectively enforced. Despite considerable resistance, with the federal government subsidizing the cost of enforcement, we expect property taxes on elites to rise and remain high as long as this "democracy by the gun" persists.

The federal government's ability to protect Black voters across the entire South was never fully realized. In the other five Reconstruction states – Alabama, Georgia, North Carolina, Texas, and Virginia – the Republican Party never gained a stronghold. Following the first set of Reconstruction elections, the Democratic Party always held at least one chamber of the legislature or the governor's office until the Democratic Party regained complete control. We call these five states the *Mixed Control* Reconstruction states. In these states, where the Democratic Party always retained enough power to protect planters, we do not expect taxation to rise much at all, and certainly to be significantly lower than in the five *Republican Control* Reconstruction states.

Last, we call the four Southern states that were not subject to the Reconstruction Acts (i.e., were not placed under military rule, were not required to write new state constitutions, retained federal representation) the *non-Reconstruction* states. As with the *Mixed Control* states, we do not expect property taxes to increase in *non-Reconstruction* states during the Reconstruction period.

The federal government's ability to enforce Black political rights in the South fell precipitously following the congressional elections of 1874, as Democrats won a majority in the federal House of Representatives for the first time since the onset of the Civil War. Democrats used this majority to block further military appropriations for Reconstruction.[71] The Compromise of 1877, which gave the Republicans the presidency in exchange for, among other promises, a commitment to remove troops engaged in enforcing Reconstruction, ended the remaining federal efforts to protect Black voters (Foner 2014). The end of any federal commitment to enforce Black political rights coincided with the loss of political control by Republicans in the last few Reconstruction states

---

[71] The Supreme Court dealt additional blows to Congressional Reconstruction through several rulings that limited the federal government's ability to prosecute violations of the Fourteenth Amendment (Foner 2014). See, for instance, *United States* v. *Cruikshank* (1876).

(e.g., Florida, South Carolina) and with the slow convergence of property taxation across all three sets of states.

Our argument predicts that under the conditions observed in the post-Reconstruction period, we should no longer see increases in property taxes. While Southern elites, through the Democratic Party, regained power, especially relative to Reconstruction, their hold on power remained contested and future political control was uncertain. Although substantially weakened by the increasingly unfettered ability of Southern Democrats to use violence and electoral fraud, Blacks formally retained the franchise and in practice remained politically active (Kousser 1974; Tolnay and Beck 1995). Non-Democratic candidates and parties still contested and occasionally even won elections in some states in the immediate post-Reconstruction period (1877–90). Furthermore, federal politics could shift in a way that supported interventions to enforce Black political rights. In this setting of contested and uncertain control on power, we expect that elites will not have incentives to support increases in property taxation.

At the same time, the coercive taxation framework predicts that in the absence of external enforcement, not only are tax increases unlikely, but we should actually see a collapse in the ability of the state to extract. This is precisely what we observe with the end of federal intervention, when property tax rates in occupied states reverted to pre-Reconstruction levels.[72]

5.1.2 Analysis

We again start with graphical evidence of our claim that on average the military occupation of the ten Reconstruction states (RS) led to higher progressive property taxation than what was observed in the four non-Reconstruction states (NRS). We then distinguish between states where the Republican Party gained unified political control and those where party control was mixed, in order to evaluate whether these groups displayed differential trajectories.

We first examine whether the presence of federal troops affected property tax trends. Figures 22 and 23 respectively present property taxes PWC and as a share of output, and Figure 24 presents ad valorem rates across the ten RS and four NRS. The vertical lines show the year in which the Democratic Party

---

[72] Suryanarayan and White (2021) provide an alternative explanation to the coercive taxation model for the observed decline in fiscal revenue following Reconstruction. The authors argue that in societies with high status inequality, high-rank groups may not only change fiscal policy but also seek to undermine the state's bureaucratic capacity as a means of blocking future redistribution. Rather than emphasizing the consequences of the removal of federal enforcement, their argument highlights status and economic inequality as the key factors explaining the uneven decline in taxation across Confederate counties in the aftermath of Reconstruction.

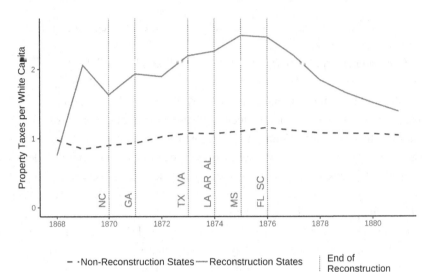

Figure 22 Property taxes per White capita (real $), 1868–1880
Reconstruction versus non-Reconstruction states (three-year moving average)

Figure 23 Property taxes/total output (agriculture and manufacturing),
1868–1880 Reconstruction versus non-Reconstruction states (three-year
moving average)

regained unified control in each state (i.e., "Redemption" in the language of
Southern Democrats). As these figures illustrate, although both groups started
off with similar levels of taxation in the immediate aftermath of the war, property taxes rose substantially more among the Reconstruction states, while trends
remained relatively stable over time in comparison states.

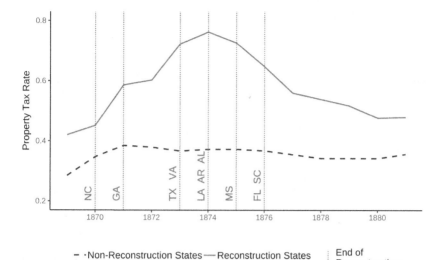

- ·Non-Reconstruction States ——Reconstruction States ⫶ End of Reconstruction

Figure 24 Property tax rate, 1868–1880 Reconstruction versus non-Reconstruction states (three-year moving average)

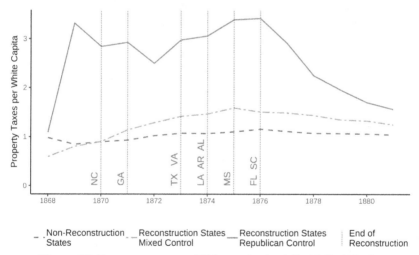

- .Non-Reconstruction
  States   _ _ Reconstruction States
  Mixed Control   __ Reconstruction States
  Republican Control   ⫶ End of
  Reconstruction

Figure 25 Property taxes per White capita (real $), 1868–1880 by Reconstruction status and party control (three-year moving average)

We now separate states into three groups: the five *Republican Control* Reconstruction states, five *Mixed Control* Reconstruction states, and four *non-Reconstruction* states. Their trajectories are shown in Figures 25, 26, and 27. In accordance with our theoretical expectations, almost all of the increase in property taxes observed among Reconstruction states in the previous figures can be attributed to the five states in which Republicans were able to achieve unified political control for multiple consecutive electoral cycles.

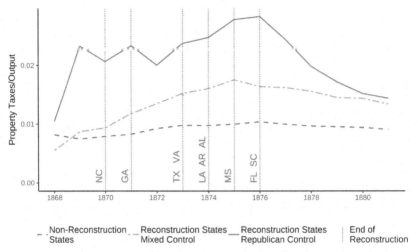

Figure 26 Property taxes/total output (agricultural and manufacturing), 1868–1880 by Reconstruction status and party control (three-year moving average)

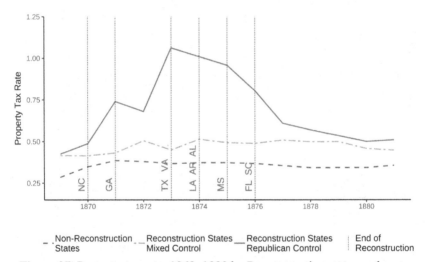

Figure 27 Property tax rate, 1868–1880 by Reconstruction status and party control (three-year moving average)

To further investigate the association between Reconstruction status and property taxation between 1868 and 1880, we adopt the following two-way fixed-effects model:

$$y_{it} = \beta_1 R_{it} + \beta_2 \mathbf{X}_{it} + \lambda_i + \gamma_t + \epsilon_{it}, \qquad (2)$$

where y_{it} is a state-level measure of property tax revenues or ad valorem rates, for state i at time t. R_{it} is an indicator variable that takes the value 1 if state i is

Table 6 Postwar period: Property taxes and Reconstruction status

	Dependent variable		
	Property taxes per White capita (real $)		
	(1)	(2)	(3)
Reconstruction Status	0.385*	0.407***	0.421**
	(0.204)	(0.155)	(0.209)
State fixed effects	Yes	Yes	Yes
Year fixed effects	Yes	Yes	Yes
Geographic covariate	Yes	Yes	Yes
Time-varying covariates	No	Yes	No
Time-invariant covariates	No	No	Yes
Observations	306	306	306
R^2	0.332	0.474	0.521

Note: Dependent variable measured as three-year moving average. All specifications account for share of enslaved population, state area, and population size (log) in 1860. Time-varying covariates included in column 2 are: state population (log), urban population (log), and agricultural and manufacturing output (log). Column 3 includes the same covariates measured in 1860 (pretreatment) interacted with year indicators. We test for the potential influence of negative weights, as proposed by de Chaisemartin and D'Haultfoeuille (2020), and find that all of our ATT receive a positive weight. $^*p<0.1$; $^{**}p<0.05$; $^{***}p<0.01$.

occupied by federal military forces in year t, and 0 otherwise. Both dependent and independent variables are measured as three-year moving averages. X_{it} represents a vector of time-varying covariates, while λ_i and γ_t represent state and year fixed effects.

Table 6 presents our baseline results for this period. As our theory predicts, federal intervention is associated with a significant increase in property taxes PWC. Table 7 further breaks down this result by differentiating between the five *Republican Control* states (i.e, where Republicans had unified control [governor plus both chambers of the legislature] for several consecutive electoral cycles), and the five *Mixed Control* Reconstruction states (i.e., those where the Republican Party lacked unified control for consecutive cycles).[73]

---

[73] To address concerns about *Reconstruction Status* or *Republican Control* being correlated with other factors that could influence taxation trajectories, in Appendix Figure A5 we conduct balance tests over a number of state-level characteristics relevant to this period. Predictably, the only significant difference relates to the share of enslaved population in RS versus NRS.

Table 7 Post Civil War period: Property taxes, Reconstruction status, and party control

	Dependent variable		
	Property taxes per White capita (real $)		
	(1)	(2)	(3)
Reconstruction and	−0.164	0.111	−0.027
Mixed Party Control	(0.265)	(0.139)	(0.171)
Reconstruction and	1.054***	0.802***	1.236***
Full Republican Control	(0.359)	(0.296)	(0.291)
State fixed effects	Yes	Yes	Yes
Year fixed effects	Yes	Yes	Yes
Geographic covariate	Yes	Yes	Yes
Time-varying covariates	No	Yes	No
Time-invariant covariates	No	No	Yes
Observations	306	306	306
R^2	0.422	0.495	0.596

Note: Dependent variable measured as three-year moving average. All specifications account for share of enslaved population, state area, and population size (log) in 1860. Time-varying covariates included in column 2 are: state population (log), urban population (log), and agricultural and manufacturing output (log). Column 3 includes the same covariates measured in 1860 (pretreatment) interacted with year indicators. The omitted category is *Non-Reconstruction*. Wald tests reveal that we can reject the null hypothesis that the coefficients for *Mixed* and *Full Republican* control are equal. $^*p<0.1$; $^{**}p<0.05$; $^{***}p<0.01$.

To assuage concerns that the Reconstruction variable may simply be picking up variation in the proportion of the newly enfranchised electorate across states, all specifications account for the share of the enslaved population in 1860. As the results show, the effect of Reconstruction on property taxes is much greater in states where the elite-dominated Democratic Party was fully removed from power than in those states where Democrats were still able to formally influence policymaking.

One obvious question regards what drove Republican control across states. Chacón et al. (2021) show, using a county-level panel, that for a given set of structural characteristics that shaped demands for redistribution (including the size of the formerly enslaved population), the local proximity of federal troops increased the electoral success of Republican state legislators. In Appendix Table A4, we show that this pattern also holds at the state level.

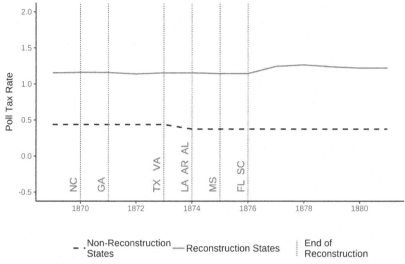

Figure 28 Poll tax rate, 1868–1880 Reconstruction versus
non-reconstruction states

A related concern is that our analysis may suffer from omitted variable bias. Suryanarayan and White (2021), for example, have shown that within Confederate states, the hollowing out of the state's administrative apparatus in the post-Reconstruction period was stronger in formerly high-slavery counties where intra-White inequality was higher. To account for the possibility that these two factors varied systematically with Republican Party control within the Confederate sample, we include both the share of the enslaved population in 1860 and intra-White inequality in 1850 as covariates, which we interact with year indicators to capture differences in trajectories across states (Table A5). Our results remain unchanged, suggesting that slavery, intra-white inequality, and Republican control influenced taxation outcomes through independent channels.

A final concern might be that the observed patterns reflect different trends in overall revenues across states, rather than an expansion in elite taxation. Using the same approach we used to investigate this possibility during the antebellum period, we look at the trajectories of poll taxes across RS and NRS. As Figure 28 shows, there is no evidence of significant changes in non-property taxation across both groups of states during this period.

5.1.3 State Spending on Common Schools

Last, we provide evidence that RS and, in particular, states with full Republican control, not only levied significantly higher property taxes during the

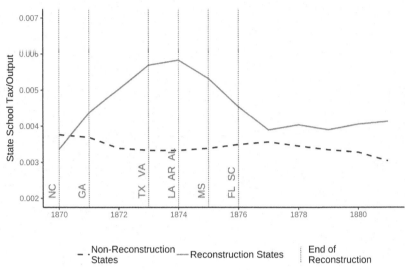

Figure 29 State taxation for common schools/total output, 1870–1880 Reconstruction versus non-Reconstruction states (three-year moving average)

occupation period, but they also spent significantly more on redistributive public goods preferred by Blacks and poorer Whites. As with property taxes, we expect spending in these states to decline with the end of Reconstruction. Given the absence of significant political changes in the NRS, and the contested nature of political power in the *Mixed Control* states, we should observe less variation in education spending during or after the end of Reconstruction across these two groups.

To test this argument, we collect the amount of either state taxes devoted to common schools or state spending from general revenues allocated toward public schools annually between 1870 and 1910, taken from state reports of the superintendent of public education (see Appendix B for sources).

Figure 29 illustrates the trends in state taxes allocated to common schools across RS and NRS. State revenues devoted to common schools as a share of output expanded markedly throughout the first half of the 1870s among the states that underwent Reconstruction, only to fall abruptly following removal of federal troops.[74]

In Figure 30, we distinguish between states where the Republican Party had unified control of state government for consecutive terms and those where the Democratic Party retained some representation. The evidence is consistent with

---

[74] Due to the admittance of Black children to public schools, we no longer normalize public education revenues by White population in the postwar period.

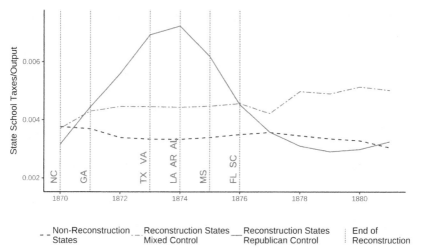

Figure 30 State taxation for common schools/total output, 1870–1880 by Reconstruction status and party control (three-year moving average)

the theoretical expectation that fiscal resources devoted to common schools as a share of output saw a substantial increase in states dominated by the Republican Party, while remaining largely unchanged in the other two groups of states. With the end of federal Reconstruction, however, this exceptional bout of growth was replaced by a period of steep decline in state school revenues among RS, which again contrasts with the trends observed in the NRS and *Mixed Control* states, where school taxes as a share of output remained generally stable during the same period.

5.2 Jim Crow: Formal Black Disenfranchisement (1880–1910)

5.2.1 Context

While the redistributive threat posed by the Republican Reconstruction governments had been eliminated by 1877, adult Black males formally retained the right to vote. In the years after Reconstruction, non-Democratic Party candidates for governor and the state legislature continued to receive substantial shares of the vote in many Southern states.[75] Of particular concern to Southern

---

[75] Far from the 'One-Party South' it would become in the twentieth century, the period between 1880 and 1900 saw opposition parties routinely win more than a third of the state legislative seats. Prior to adoption of suffrage restrictions on Blacks, non-Democratic Party candidates routinely won more than 40 percent of the popular vote for governor: Alabama (three out of ten elections), Arkansas (five/seven), Florida (three/three), Georgia (two/ten), Louisiana (two/four), Mississippi (one/three), North Carolina (six/six), South Carolina (zero/eight), Tennessee (ten/ten), Texas (four/ten), Virginia (four/five) (Dubin 2010).

elites, cross-racial class-based ("fusion") coalitions had successfully formed to win control of state governments in Virginia (early 1880s) and North Carolina (mid-1890s), and had nearly won in several other states (Perman 2003).

While the durability of such coalitions was never demonstrated during this period, the mere possibility posed a particular threat to Southern elites. Like many rural societies based on coerced labor, the US South during the 1880s was characterized by high land inequality, fiscal retrenchment, and low spending on broad public goods, especially public education (Alston and Ferrie 2007; Margo 2007; Galor et al. 2009; Vollrath 2013; Suryanarayan and White 2021). The increase in regressive taxation and retrenchment in public spending that emerged in the post-Reconstruction period engendered significant resentment among poorer Whites and fueled the populist and cross-racial fusion movements that threatened Southern Democratic Party dominance (Kousser 1974; Hyman 1989; Hahn 2006).

These electoral threats to Democratic Party rule ended with the adoption by eleven states of various suffrage restrictions, such as poll taxes and literacy tests, between 1889 and 1906 (Perman 2003; Valelly 2009).[76] While not explicitly racial in nature, these restrictions removed the formal voting eligibility of substantial portions of the Black electorate.[77] The historical record is clear that elites saw White supremacy as crucial for maintaining Democratic Party hegemony. To take just one example, a delegate to the 1898 Louisiana constitutional convention, which adopted poll taxes and a literacy test, said: "What is the state? It is the Democratic Party ... We meet here to establish the supremacy of the white race, and the white race constitutes the Democratic Party of this state." The effects of these restrictions on lower-income Whites is less known. While 'Grandfather' clauses and other similar mechanisms were adopted to maintain White voter suffrage, turnout and likely voter eligibility of lower-income Whites declined (Kousser 1974).

Our argument suggests that in the post-Reconstruction period, during which political contestation to Democratic Party elite rule remained and future control was uncertain, we should expect declining and/or low levels of progressive property taxation. If franchise restrictions led to tighter elite control *and* elites demanded some collective goods, we should see that Black disenfranchisement resulted in higher property taxes. If, however, elite control was not coupled

---

[76] See Table 1, columns 7 and 8, for the timing and types of suffrage restrictions adopted in each state.

[77] In states that adopted literacy tests, it has been shown that Black disenfranchisement was nearly 100 percent (Keele, Cubbison, and White 2021). In states requiring the payment of the poll tax to be eligible to vote, it has been estimated that approximately half of Black voters lost their eligibility (Kousser 1974).

with demands for greater collective goods, then taxation should not rise much. As shown in what follows, states in which elite control was strongest – as measured separately by either the implementation of a literacy test (which disenfranchised most Black voters) or the Democratic Party seat share in the state legislature – had higher property taxes PWC. Spending, however, does not increase to the same extent as in the prewar period. We believe there were fewer collective goods desired by elites at this time, something that would not change appreciably until the automobile age. The key point in terms of our argument is that property taxes and spending on elite goods, such as colleges and universities, increased more in states in which the Democratic Party had greater control.

5.2.2 Analysis

We begin by visually showing the change in property taxes between 1880 and 1910 across states that adopted some type of suffrage restriction (poll tax or literacy test) versus those that did not enact any of these measures. This allows us to assess if the patterns observed among disenfranchising states diverge from the secular trends affecting all states irrespective of their voting laws.

Each category separates the states into the likely effects of Black disenfranchisement on elite political control. Literacy tests and poll taxes drastically reduced the political participation of Black voters and therefore should have provided elites with a higher degree of political control both in the present and into the future. By contrast, the absence of suffrage restrictions clearly did little to institutionally buffer elite dominance. Holding elite demand for collective goods constant, we expect property taxes in the states with poll taxes or literacy tests to increase faster (or fall less) than in the states without voting restrictions.[78]

Figure 31 shows the average property taxes PWC and as a share of output, along with ad valorem rates, for each set of states between 1880 and 1910. The dashed vertical lines in these figures denote the year in which each state adopted voting restrictions (either a poll tax or a literacy test). As the first figure shows, property taxes PWC increased rapidly, on average, among states that implemented suffrage restrictions and remained largely unchanged in comparison states. As a share of output (Figure 31b), property taxes fell markedly and continuously among non-Restriction states while showing a less pronounced decrease among disenfranchising states. In particular, the acceleration observed

---

[78] While *No Restriction* states are clearly different in important ways (i.e., Blacks comprised a much smaller share of these states' populations), they do provide evidence that we are not simply capturing some period-specific trend.

(a) Property taxes per White capita

(b) Property taxes/output

Figure 31 Property tax outcomes by restriction status, 1880–1910

in the years after the last state (Georgia) implemented restrictive measures does not appear to be driven by common shocks affecting all states: there is no increase in states that did not adopt voting restrictions.

While the amount of property taxes levied constitutes a common measure of direct taxation on the wealthy, it may reflect both a political decision and underlying differences in states' fiscal capabilities. Because our theory seeks

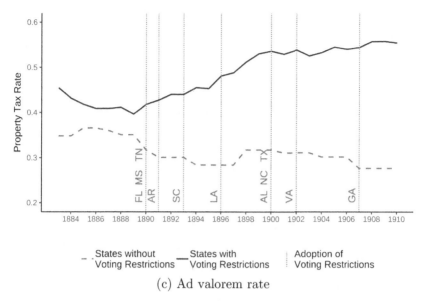

(c) Ad valorem rate

Figure 31 (continued)

to explain supply-side decisions, changes in ad valorem property tax rates provide a strong complementary test. We present these results in Figure 31c. The striking divergence is consistent with our previous findings and strengthens the credibility of our other taxation measures.

Another way of evaluating the existence of differential trends across groups of states is to look at taxation patterns based on the number of years from the implementation of suffrage restrictions. Given the staggered adoption of disenfranchising measures across states, such figures may provide a clearer depiction of the incremental divergence between Restriction and non-Restriction states. Figure 32 shows, in Black, average property taxes among states that implemented voting restrictions in the ten years before disenfranchisement and the twenty years after. The grey lines show property taxes in states that did not adopt restrictive measures. Once again, the figures show a marked divergence in property taxes between states that adopted franchise restrictions and the comparison group.[79]

To further assess our hypothesis that variation in elite control is the relevant mechanism through which poll taxes and literacy tests may influence

---

[79] Appendix Figure A6 shows the Nadaraya-Watson nonparametric regressions with Epanechnikov kernel (bandwidths chosen by rule-of-thumb estimator) of property taxes (a) PWC, (b) as a share of output, and (c) ad valorem rates with 95 percent confidence intervals.

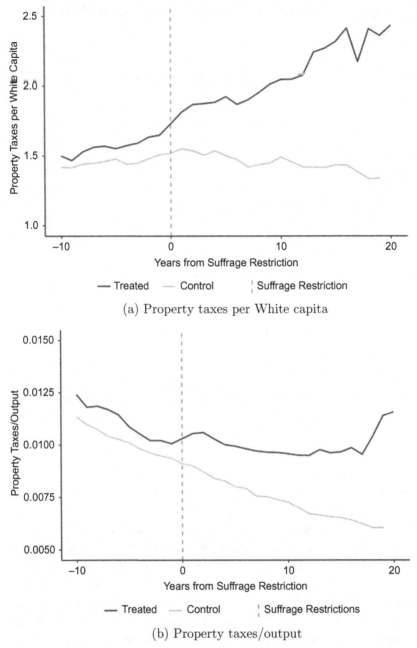

(a) Property taxes per White capita

(b) Property taxes/output

Figure 32 Property tax outcomes by disenfranchisement status ten years before and twenty years after suffrage restrictions

Note: The black lines show average (a) property taxes PWC, (b) as a share of output, and (c) ad valorem rates across states that adopted suffrage restrictions. For each state where voting restrictions were implemented in a given year, we calculate the average property taxes of a control group that is composed of all states that did not have restrictive measures in that year or before – i.e., the control group includes both never-treated and not-yet-treated units. The grey line reflects the average trend across all control groups.

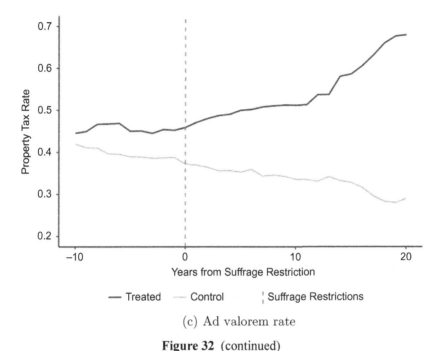

(c) Ad valorem rate

Figure 32 (continued)

property taxation, we investigate the heterogeneous effects of suffrage restrictions with respect to the level of political dominance that the Democratic Party achieved across states. Specifically, we differentiate between states where the Democratic Party had a high (i.e., above average) share of seats in the state legislature following the adoption of restrictions and those where the party's dominance was less pronounced – Arkansas, North Carolina, Tennessee, and Virginia – despite having adopted the same measures as their counterparts.

We present property taxes PWC across time by level of Democratic control in Figure 33, property taxes over output in Figure 34, and ad valorem tax rates in Figure 35. The diverging lines suggest a significant gap in taxation between the disenfranchising states where the Democratic Party dominated the legislature and both states without restrictions and those with voting restrictions but weaker Democratic control. Although the three groups display largely parallel trends before 1890, their taxation patterns begin to diverge after the first states (Florida, Mississippi, and Tennessee) adopt franchise restrictions. Overall, the figures show that Democratic-leaning states appear to experience a larger increase in property taxes PWC – and a smaller decrease in property taxes over output – than their counterparts, which we attribute to elites' increased political control and reduced uncertainty over their future ability to shape fiscal policy in these states.

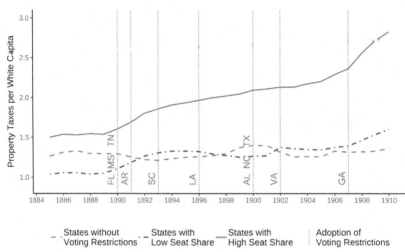

Figure 33 Property taxes per White capita (real $), 1880–1910 by disenfranchisement status and Democratic seat share (three-year moving average)

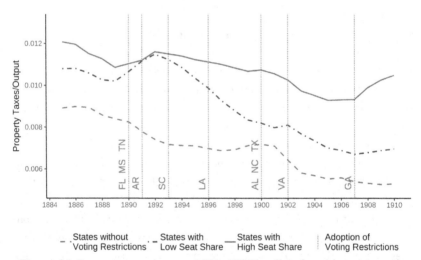

Figure 34 Property taxes/output, 1880–1910 by disenfranchisement status and Democratic seat share (three-year moving average)

5.2.3 Event Study

To further investigate whether the adoption of suffrage restrictions significantly altered the levels of progressive taxation across states, we estimate an event study model that relies on information from states without suffrage restrictions to estimate the counterfactual trend of disenfranchising states. Specifically, we rely on the estimation technique proposed by Sun and Abraham (2021),

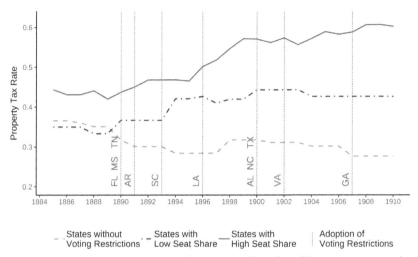

States without Voting Restrictions — · — States with Low Seat Share ——— States with High Seat Share ⋮ Adoption of Voting Restrictions

Figure 35 Property tax rate, 1880–1910 by disenfranchisement status and Democratic seat share (three-year moving average)

which is robust to treatment effect heterogeneity. This method uses a linear two-way fixed-effects specification that interacts cohort indicators with relative period indicators to estimate a weighted average of the cohort-specific average treatment effects on the treated ($CATT_{e,l}$) as follows:

$$y_{it} = \alpha_i + \lambda_t + \sum_{e} \sum_{l \neq -1} \delta_{e,l}(1\{E_i = e\} \cdot D_{it}^l) + \epsilon_{it},$$

where y_{it} is the outcome of interest for unit i at time t, E_i is the time at which unit i first receives the binary treatment, and D_{it}^l is an indicator for unit i that is l periods away from the adoption of suffrage restrictions at calendar time t.[80] Additionally, α_i accounts for fixed-state characteristics that influence taxation levels and the probability of suffrage restrictions being adopted, while λ_t accounts for any common temporal shocks affecting all states. Under the identifying assumptions of no anticipation and parallel trends, the coefficient estimator $\widehat{\delta}_{e,l}$ is a DID estimator for $CATT_{e,l}$.[81]

The results shown in Figure 36 are consistent with our theory: suffrage restrictions were followed by an expansion of property taxes that exceeded what is observed in states that did not adopt restrictive measures. Figure 36a shows the average estimated effect on property taxes of voting restrictions for

---

[80] For never-treated units $E_i = \infty$, and $D_{it}^l = 0$, for all l and all t.

[81] In settings with treatment effect heterogeneity and variation in treatment timing, two-way fixed-effects models can yield estimates that do not capture the dynamic treatment effect and may reflect spurious terms comprising treatment effects from other periods (see, e.g., de Chaisemartin and D'Haultfoeuille 2022).

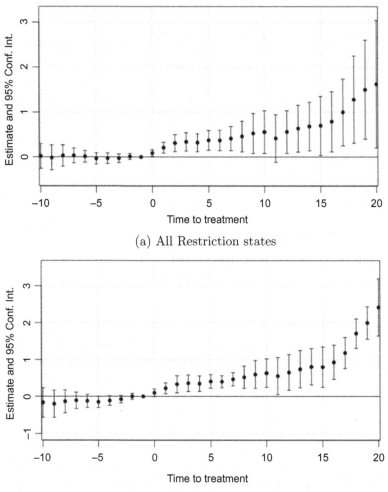

(a) All Restriction states

(b) States with high Democratic seat share

Figure 36 Event study estimate of the effect of suffrage restrictions on property taxes per White capita, ten years before and and twenty years after disenfranchisement

Note: Point estimates and 95 percent confidence intervals for the effect of suffrage restrictions on property taxes PWC, based on an event study model estimated for the ten years preceding and the twenty years following the adoption of voting restrictions. Standard errors are clustered at the state level. Figure (a) comprises all states. Figure (b) shows the effect of suffrage restrictions among states where the Democratic Party had an above-average seat share in the legislature. Estimates ten years or more after treatment should be interpreted cautiously, as the sample size decreases over time.

all disenfranchising states (regardless of party dominance), and 95 percent confidence intervals from standard errors clustered at the state level. Figure 36b shows the average estimated effect of voting restrictions for the eleven states with above-average Democratic Party seat share in the legislature.

These figures highlight three central findings. First, the estimated coefficients for $l > 0$ suggest that following the adoption of suffrage restrictions, disenfranchising states experienced a progressive increase in property taxes PWC that surpassed the trajectory of states without restrictive measures. Second, the estimated coefficients for the pretreatment period are statistically indistinguishable from zero, adding credibility to the identifying assumptions. Third, the estimated long-term effect of disenfranchisement on property taxation is substantively large: restrictions increased property taxes by $0.55 PWC within ten years of disenfranchisement, which represents a 33 percent increase from the pre-restriction average of 1.65. Among the sample of states dominated by the Democratic Party, the expansion in property taxes is even larger, reaching a 39 percent increase from the pre-restriction average over the same period. Appendix Figure A7 shows the same analysis using property taxes as a share of output as the dependent variable. The substantive results remain unchanged.

Taken together, these results provide support for the argument that suffrage restrictions were a critical determinant of the expansion of property taxation among Southern states in the early twentieth century. Nonetheless, a few limitations are worth highlighting. First, it is difficult to ascertain if these estimates reflect a causal effect of suffrage restrictions. Important correlates of taxation, such as those highlighted by Suryanarayan and White (2021) – namely, the level of intra-White inequality or administrative capacity – might be systematically associated with disenfranchisement and thus account for our results. We investigate this possibility and find no significant pretreatment differences across disenfranchising and non-disenfranchising states (Figure A8a). Similarly, we find the level of legislative control exerted by the Democratic Party across disenfranchising states to be unrelated to pre–Jim Crow levels of intra-White inequality and state capacity (Figure A8b). To further assuage concerns that *Restriction* and *non-Restriction* states are fundamentally different, we carry out additional analyses implementing the Callaway and Sant'Anna (2021) estimator, which uses future-treated states as control units in their pretreatment years. The results, presented in Appendix Figure A9, again show a positive impact of suffrage restrictions on property taxes PWC, taxes as a share of output, and ad valorem rates. Appendix Figure A10, in turn, shows that our findings are robust to the DIDm estimator proposed by de Chaisemartin and D'Haultfoeuille (2020). The DIDm estimator allows us to

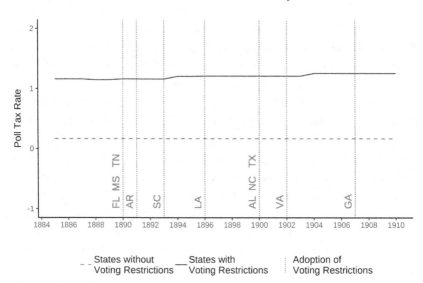

Figure 37 Poll tax rate, 1880–1910 by disenfranchisement status (three-year moving average)

control for state-specific linear time trends and for intra-White inequality (and bureaucratic capacity) interacted with time-fixed effects.

A second potential concern is that the differential trends we observe in property taxes over time may simply reflect a larger effort of *Restriction* states to increase total revenues (i.e., through all types of tax instruments), rather than a phenomenon restricted to progressive taxes. If this is the case, we would expect to see the same pattern of divergence in more regressive forms of taxation, such as poll taxes. This is not what the evidence shows: states that adopted voting restrictions levy higher property taxes than their counterparts, while maintaining their poll tax rates largely unchanged – their trend is parallel to that observed in *non-Restriction states* throughout the whole period. The trajectories shown in Figure 37 thus provide support for the idea that even though elites favored increasing property taxes in *Restriction* states, they refrained from raising the fiscal burden of other societal groups.

Finally, readers might also wonder about the plausibility of an alternative interpretation to our results. Specifically, the concomitant growth of urban areas and rates of industrialization during this period raise the question of whether increases in revenue resulted from expanding property values of urban assets, rather than an increased burden on landed elites. This may have been the case if, for instance, landed elites used property value assessments as a means of shifting the tax burden to the manufacturing sector. Mares and Queralt (2015) have found support for this idea in the Prussian setting, where intra-elite conflict was shown to have prompted the support for and development of increased fiscal extraction. To investigate this possibility, we gathered data on property value assessments across eight states from 1885 to 1910 – seven *Restriction* states and the *non-Restriction* state of Missouri.[82] We then subtract from total assessed property values the amount related to rural land to create a variable that represents the share of non-rural land property values. The idea is that if non-land assets were disproportionately increasing in value over time, then this would suggest that property taxes were increasingly borne by non-rural actors. Using the Sun and Abraham (2021) approach adopted in the foregoing analyses, we investigate whether voting restrictions were associated with a differential increase in urban or industrial taxable property values. We find no evidence in support of this mechanism in our setting: not only do we not see any systematic relationship between disenfranchisement and the share of non-land property value (Figure 38), we also fail to find a positive association between this measure and property taxes collected in our two-way fixed-effects specifications – in fact, if anything, this association appears to be negative (see Table 8).

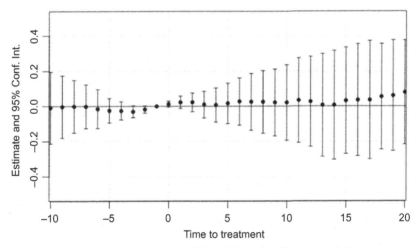

Figure 38 Event study estimate of the effect of suffrage restrictions on the share of non-land property value

Note: Point estimates and 95 percent confidence intervals for the effect of suffrage restrictions on the non-land share of property values, based on an event study model estimated for the ten years before and the twenty years after restrictions are adopted. Standard errors clustered at the state level.

---

[82] Unfortunately, this information was only available for this restricted sample of states.

Table 8 Non-land share of property value and property taxes collected, 1885–1910

	Dependent variable		
	Total property taxes, real $ (log)		
	(1)	(2)	(3)
Non-land property value (%)	0.364	−0.836	−2.202**
	(0.497)	(0.724)	(0.961)
Additional covariates	No	Yes	Yes
Time-varying covariates	No	Yes	No
Time-invariant covariates	No	No	Yes
Observations	248	248	248
R^2	0.105	0.366	0.718

Note: Main variables measured as three-year moving averages. Covariates included are: state population (log), urban population (log), and total output (log). All specifications include state area interacted with year indicators. Column 2 includes time-varying covariates, and column 3 includes the same covariates but measured in 1880 (pretreatment) interacted with year indicators. $p<0.1$; $p<0.05$; $p<0.01$.

5.2.4 State Spending on Common Schools versus Universities

Last, we check for evidence on whether this increase in property taxation was allocated toward redistributive goods or elite collective goods. We choose one good of each type: state spending on common schools represents our measure of redistributive expenditure and state spending on colleges and universities is our measure of a collective good that is preferred by elites.[83] We expect states where the Democratic Party has firmer control (which is likely to persist due to the adoption of suffrage restrictions) to increase their spending on universities but not necessarily on common schools. For spending on universities, we located the itemized list of total disbursements from each state's report of auditor, treasurer, or comptroller. Combined with our previously described measure of state spending on common schools, we have good coverage (each state typically has at least one value every three years between 1880 and 1910).

---

[83] We do not focus on railroads after the Civil War because we do not have the same clean breakdown of expenditures. It is also worth noting that the nature of railroad financing changed after the Civil War, with direct state support becoming much less relevant vis-à-vis the federal government and private inflows (notably from the North) (Goodrich 1974).

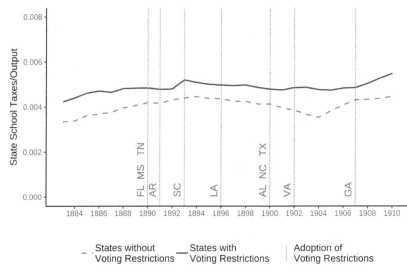

Figure 39 State spending on common schools/output, 1880–1910 by disenfranchisement status (three-year moving average)

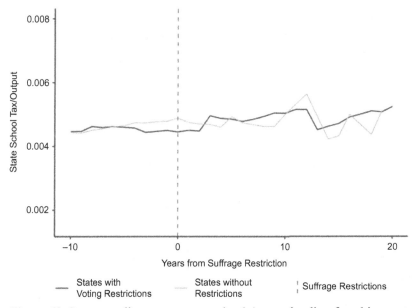

Figure 40 State spending on common schools/output by disenfranchisement status ten years before and twenty years after suffrage restrictions

Figure 39 illustrates the trends in state taxes devoted to common schools across disenfranchising and non-disenfranchising states. Figure 40 shows average school taxes as a share of output among states that adopted voting restrictions in the ten years before their implementation and the twenty years after,

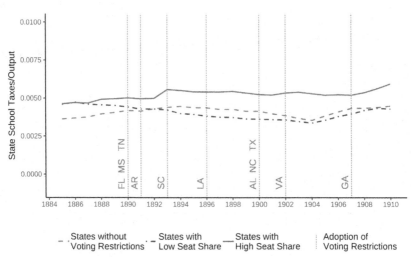

Figure 41 State spending on common schools/output, 1880–1910 by disenfranchisement status and Democratic Party control (three-year moving average)

and compares them to the trends observed among the control group – that is, all states that did not have voting restrictions in place in any given year.[84] The evidence provides support for the expectation that state taxes devoted to schools as a share of output did not differ systematically across the two groups of states, which maintained parallel trajectories throughout the whole period. In contrast to the Reconstruction era, and consistent with our theoretical expectations, these results show that unlike the trends observed in property taxes, expenditure patterns on redistributive goods did not diverge systematically across disenfranchising and comparison states during the Jim Crow period. In other words, the expanded fiscal resources restriction states obtained through property taxation were not proportionally allocated to the provision of broad-access public goods.

In Figure 41, we distinguish between restriction states where the Democratic Party had a higher-than-average share of seats in the state legislature versus those where the Democratic Party had a weaker grip on power, and those that never implemented voting restrictions. Again, we see no systematic divergence in allocations for common schools over time across the three groups of states. These figures provide further support for the idea that regardless of the level of Democratic dominance, and despite the increase in taxation that occurred in some states during this period, redistributive spending as a share of output

---

[84] Figure A11 in the Appendix shows the Nadaraya-Watson regressions.

remained relatively stable throughout the whole period across the three groups of states.

By contrast, state spending on selective public goods related to elite education experienced a remarkably different trajectory. Exploring the temporal variation in state spending on colleges and universities, we investigate whether elites in disenfranchising states were willing to progressively increase the amount of public resources allocated to the provision of this type of *selective* public good.[85] Figure 42 shows average college spending PWC and as a share of output among states that adopted voting restrictions in the ten years before the implementation and the twenty years after, together with the trends of the comparison group.[86] Figure 43 shows divergent trends in college spending across non-restriction states and disenfranchising states – distinguishing between those where the Democratic Party had a higher versus lower share of seats in the legislature. While spending PWC and as a share of output stagnated (or increased only mildly) in non-restriction states, it experienced gradual and sustained increase among restriction states, especially in those controlled by the Democratic Party.

Overall, together with the evidence on taxes destined to common schools, these results provide support for the idea that after disenfranchisement, elites raised property taxes in the states where they had greater political control and spent the increased public resources on the provision of selective (rather than redistributive) public goods. Our results stand in contrast to Lieberman (2003), who finds that in South Africa "the push from white lower groups" led upper-class groups to accept an increase in progressive taxation and redistributive spending that benefited low-income Whites.

Conclusion

This Element explains patterns of fiscal development in the American South from 1820–1910. Our theoretical discussion contrasted exchange and coercion-based models of taxes and spending, and drilled down on the particular challenges of taxing agricultural elites in highly unequal societies. We argued that the willingness of the plantation class to comply with tax demands would in substantial part determine the amount of taxes raised, the costs of enforcement,

---

[85] Spending on White universities and colleges includes spending on medical schools and technical, engineering schools, but excludes teaching colleges – then called normal schools or industrial schools; it also excludes all federal spending on schools, as well as state spending on Black colleges and universities.

[86] Figure A12 in the Appendix shows the Nadaraya-Watson regressions.

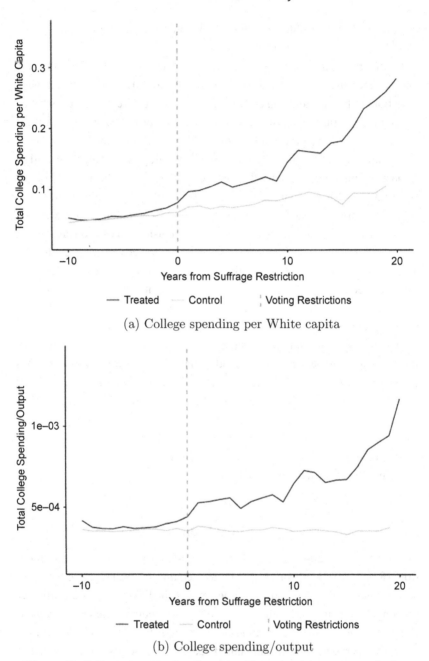

(a) College spending per White capita

(b) College spending/output

Figure 42 College spending by disenfranchisement status ten years before
and twenty years after suffrage restrictions

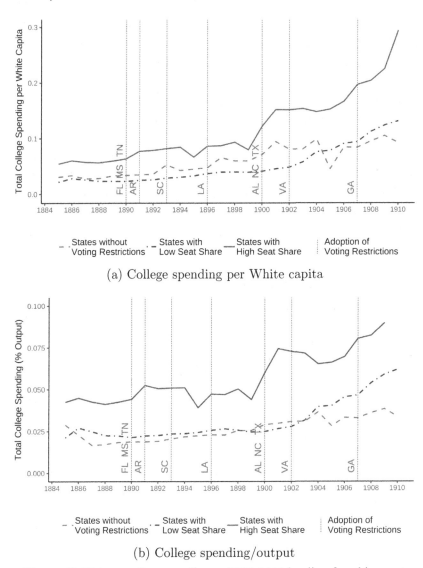

(a) College spending per White capita

(b) College spending/output

Figure 43 State spending on colleges, 1880–1910 by disenfranchisement status and Democratic Party control (three-year moving average)

and the sustainability of the fiscal pathway. We then laid out specific conditions under which agricultural elites would accept (or resist) taxation: landed elites would support taxation if and only if they covet collective goods from the state, have a monopoly on political power in the present, and also believe this monopoly will persist. These conditions allow them to benefit from public spending today, while ensuring that the enhanced extractive powers of the state will not be used against them later.

We then assessed the explanatory power of these models using original, archival data with relatively comprehensive coverage of state-level taxes and spending from 1820–1910. Our analysis pinned down the incidence of taxation and the distribution of spending, leveraged shocks that changed elite power and preferences at critical moments, and identified the political developments and institutional mechanisms that influenced the trajectory of these fiscal outcomes over time.

In brief, we find that both broad models of public finance help us understand the evolution of taxation and spending across Southern states from 1820 to 1910. Consistent with the theoretical conjectures, the quasi-voluntary periods were prevalent, lucrative, and self-sustaining; the coercion model briefly proved capable of raising significant amount of revenue, but it also triggered significant resistance, which probably contributed endogenously to its own demise. Because it relied on third-party enforcement, it proved ephemeral once this external (federal) enforcement was removed. We find strong support for our hypothesis about elite behavior with respect to taxes and spending and the institutions governing these fiscal outcomes across all three periods and across different constellations of spatial variation in planter power.

Among the specific findings, we highlight the following: during the antebellum period, half of the Southern states were malapportioned in ways that provided the plantation elites an enduring lock on power; the other half were not malapportioned, meaning that the majority of poor Whites could always pose a redistributive threat. When a common economic shock from roughly 1844 to 1860 raised the value of slaves and cash crops throughout the South, it triggered significantly different fiscal responses. In MS, governments raised taxes on the agricultural elites and plowed it back into railroads, thereby increasing the net wealth of the plantation class. In NMS, by contrast, legislatures were unable to agree to raise taxes or fund railroads. The tax-railroad gap between MS and NMS only changed when existing political institutions were altered by Reconstruction.

The Civil War temporarily diminished the power of the plantation class throughout the South. As in the prewar period, however, there was spatial and temporal variation, determined in this case by the extent of Northern occupation. Places with more Northern troops had more coercive power. They elected more Black officials and Republicans, raised more from property taxes, and spent more progressively.

The presidential election of 1876 heralded the North's final retreat from Southern politics, though the threat of Northern intervention persisted until the 1890s. While planter elites were able to reassert their power over Southern politics, their ability to secure their hold on power (that is, to create an enduring lock) was limited until they enacted voting restrictions that reduced Black, and to a lesser extent poor White, electoral participation. In places with more restrictions, the Democratic Party reigned supreme, triggering a rise in progressive taxes and spending on goods that disproportionately favored White elites, notably universities.

In short, we find that the plantation class embraced taxes on themselves whenever and wherever they unambiguously called the shots politically, had institutional mechanisms that locked in their power, and desired collective goods. In places where they were neither completely dominant, nor well protected against future reversals in power, elite taxation stalled. In places where their political power was effectively restricted (primarily due to federal enforcement of lower-class political rights), elite taxation surged. As external enforcement dissipated, property taxes collapsed. Our finding about the fragile nature of coercion-induced compliance during Reconstruction echoes arguments found elsewhere. Suryanarayan and White (2021, p. 3), for example, note that "Southern white elites were able to weaken taxation and bureaucratic institutions in the Southern states, even before the enactment of institutional mechanisms such as Jim Crow and suffrage restrictions." Our general conclusion complements their findings by showing that rather than marking the end of elite taxation, the implementation of Jim Crow-era suffrage restrictions constituted the nadir of the downward trend, as elites reimposed taxes on themselves once they had successfully eliminated potential rivals.

The fact that the plantation elite increased taxation and fiscal capacity whenever they had uncontested and uncontestable power and resisted it when these conditions were missing is only one facet of our story. Another facet is that taxation of the elite seems to be unassociated with redistribution or development in a broader sense. In other words, there was no benevolence here, as taxation of the elite was essentially for the elite, with the proceeds helping sustain a repressive state and exploitative economy. Phillips (1908, p. 20), for example, claimed that "The building of railroads led to little else but the extension and intensification of the plantation system and the increase of the staple output." We believe the post-1890s increase in progressive taxation had a similar pro-wealthy White skew, as suggested by educational expenditures.

Even more interesting perhaps is the question of why Southern elites did not impose more taxes on poor Southern Whites when their control over government was unassailable. One potential explanation is that relying on other sources of revenue, such as consumption taxes, was not feasible: tax collection in agricultural economies that operate primarily through informal structures – i.e., without broad reliance on banking systems or written records of economic transactions – is costly, as enforcement consumes a large proportion of potential revenue (Moore 2008). Large-scale consumption taxes, for example, might have required better technologies, higher levels of development, and/or higher levels of urbanization (Aidt and Jensen 2009; Beramendi et al. 2019). Second, given their lack of influence over spending, lower-income Whites might have rebelled or migrated to other states if their tax burden became too high. With few incoming migrants and considerable outflows of people, particularly following the Civil War, labor scarcity was a chronic threat.[87] More importantly, perhaps, more intense taxation on non-elites could have engendered more enduring and broad-based class-based cross-race coalitions that could have upended planter political control. The fact that poll taxes really only rose substantially immediately after the Civil War, when the plantation class was at its weakest, but not when Southern elites dominated comfortably, reveals that the elite were unwilling or unable to shift taxes to groups with mobility options and without a significant voice in government.

Another question concerns the generalizability of our explanation for elite behavior and taxation and spending patterns outside of the American South. We think the conditions we have identified for rural elite support for or resistance to taxes may be generalizable. However, the necessary empirical conditions – unchallenged political control by the rural elite, no foreseeable threats to their rule, and the existence of cost-effective collective goods that directly benefit them – may be rare. The existing literature suggests that agricultural elites do not generally want collective goods from the state, an assumption that seems plausible on its face. Likewise, we can also imagine the rural class not pursuing goods that they might benefit from if the provision of such goods could set in motion social or economic changes that might threaten their rent-generation system over the long run. We further speculate that the belief that monopolies on power will persist is not widespread. In Imperial Brazil (1822–89), for example, rural elites clearly had uncontested political control in a variety of places, but whether they could exert full control over the allocation of fiscal resources is an entirely different matter. Throughout most of the nineteenth century, control over public finance was concentrated in the central government and the various regional elites had little assurance that they (rather than other groups) would benefit from the way in which taxes were used. This limited the amount of resources that they were willing to accord to the government (Leff 1997, p. 55). Overall, we suspect that taxation of the rich, by the rich, for the rich might be more likely in hybrid regimes that limit both the political power of the masses and the centralization of power in an unelected ruler. In

---

[87] The 1900 Census counted more than 1 million Southern-born Whites and 335,000 Blacks living outside the South; both figures would roughly double by 1920 (Gregory 2006, p. 15).

Apartheid-era South Africa for example, progressive taxation accompanied and undergirded mass repression. Clearly, much more could be done to assess the extent to which our explanation travels to other settings.

In short, this Element has both revealed heretofore unknown fiscal patterns in the American South during the nineteenth century and introduced a novel explanation for the emergence of elite taxation with a specific set of institutions and economic conditions. Our findings suggest an important twist on the fiscal contract adage of "no taxation without representation." For the rich, "no taxation if others have (or might obtain) representation" may be more appropriate. We think our study's basic organizing principles – taxes and public spending should go together; they are linked by mechanisms of representation; and deviations from this tripartite structure are likely to generate attempts to change the institutions that govern representation and fiscal policy – should inform the comparative literature on the development of fiscal systems elsewhere.

References

Acemoglu, Daron, Suresh Naidu, Pascual Restrepo, and James Robinson. 2015. "Democracy, redistribution, and inequality." In *Handbook of income distribution*. Vol. 2. Elsevier, pp. 1885–1966.

Acemoglu, Daron, and James Robinson. 2006. "De facto political power and institutional persistence." *American Economic Review* 96(2): 325–330.

Aidt, Toke, and Peter Jensen. 2009. "Tax structure, size of government, and the extension of the voting franchise in Western Europe, 1860–1938." *International Tax and Public Finance* 16(3): 362–394.

Albertus, Michael, and Victor Menaldo. 2014. "Gaming democracy: Elite dominance during transition and the prospects for redistribution." *British Journal of Political Science* 44(3): 575–603.

Alston, Lee, and Joseph Ferrie. 2007. *Southern paternalism and the American welfare state: Economics, politics, and institutions in the South, 1865–1965*. Cambridge University Press.

Ansell, Ben, and David Samuels. 2014. *Inequality and democratization: An elite-competition approach*. Cambridge University Press.

Atack, Jeremy. 2015. "Historical Geographic Information Systems (GIS) database of steamboat-navigated rivers during the nineteenth century in the United States." https://my.vanderbilt.edu/jeremyatack/data-downloads.

Bateman, David, Ira Katznelson, and John Lapinski. 2018. *Southern nation: Congress and White supremacy after reconstruction*. Princeton University Press.

Baten, Joerg, and Ralph Hippe. 2018. "Geography, land inequality and regional numeracy in Europe in historical perspective." *Journal of Economic Growth* 23(1): 79–109.

Bates, Robert, and Da-Hsiang Lien. 1985. "A note on taxation, development, and representative government." *Politics & Society* 14(1): 53–70.

Beramendi, Pablo, Mark Dincecco, and Melissa Rogers. 2019. "Intra-elite competition and long-run fiscal development." *Journal of Politics* 81(1): 49–65.

Beramendi, Pablo, and Jeffrey L. Jensen. 2019. "Economic geography, political inequality, and public goods in the original 13 US states." *Comparative Political Studies* 52(13–14): 2235–2282.

Bernstein, Thomas, and Xiaobo Lü. 2003. *Taxation without representation in contemporary rural China*. Cambridge University Press.

Besley, Timothy, and Torsten Persson. 2011. *Pillars of prosperity: The political economics of development clusters*. Princeton University Press.

Boix, Carles. 2003. *Democracy and redistribution*. Cambridge University Press.

Callaway, Brantly, and Pedro H. C. Sant'Anna. 2021. "Difference-in-differences with multiple time periods." *Journal of Econometrics* 225(2): 200–230. www.sciencedirect.com/science/article/pii/S0304407620303948.

Chacón, Mario, and Jeffrey L. Jensen. 2020a. "Direct democracy, constitutional reform, and political inequality in Post-colonial America." *Studies in American Political Development* 34(1): 148–169.

Chacón, Mario, and Jeffrey L. Jensen. 2020b. "Democratization, de facto power, and taxation: Evidence from military occupation during Reconstruction." *World Politics* 72(1): 1–46.

Chacón, Mario, and Jeffrey L. Jensen. 2020c. "The political and economic geography of Southern secession." *Journal of Economic History* 80(2): 386–416.

Chacón, Mario, Jeffrey L. Jensen, and Sidak Yntiso. 2021. "Sustaining democracy with force: Black representation during Reconstruction." *Journal of Historical Political Economy* 1(3): 319–351.

D'arcy, Michelle, and Marina Nistotskaya. 2018. "The early modern origins of contemporary European tax outcomes." *European Journal of Political Research* 57(1): 47–67.

de Chaisemartin, Clément, and Xavier D'Haultfoeuille. 2020. "Two-way fixed effects estimators with heterogeneous treatment effects." *American Economic Review* 110(9): 2964–2996.

de Chaisemartin, Clément, and Xavier D'Haultfoeuille. 2022. "Two-way fixed effects and differences-in-differences with heterogeneous treatment effects: A survey." NBER Working Paper 29691.

Dincecco, Mark. 2011. *Political transformations and public finances: Europe, 1650–1913*. Cambridge University Press.

Dincecco, Mark. 2017. *State capacity and economic development: Present and past*. Cambridge University Press.

Donnelly, William. 1965. "Conspiracy or popular movement: The historiography of Southern support for secession." *North Carolina Historical Review* 42(1): 70–84.

Dube, Oeindrila, and Juan Vargas. 2013. "Commodity price shocks and civil conflict: Evidence from Colombia." *Review of Economic Studies* 80(4): 1384–1421.

Dubin, Michael. 2007. *Party affiliations in the state legislatures: A year by year summary, 1796–2006.* McFarland.

Dubin, Michael. 2010. *United States gubernatorial elections, 1861–1911: The official results by state and county.* McFarland.

Egerton, Douglas. 2014. *The wars of reconstruction: The brief, violent history of America's most progressive era.* Bloomsbury.

Einhorn, Robin. 2006. *American taxation, American slavery.* University of Chicago Press.

Emmenegger, Patrick, Lucas Leemann, and André Walter. 2021. "No direct taxation without new elite representation: Industrialization and the domestic politics of taxation." *European Journal of Political Research* 60(3): 648–669.

Fishlow, Albert. 1965. *American railroads and the transformation of the antebellum economy.* Harvard University Press.

Flores-Macías, Gustavo A. 2022. *Contemporary state building.* Cambridge University Press.

Fogel, Robert. 1994. *Without consent or contract: The rise and fall of American slavery.* W. W. Norton.

Foner, Eric. 1993. *Freedom's lawmakers: A directory of Black officeholders during Reconstruction.* Oxford University Press.

Foner, Eric. 2014. *Reconstruction: America's unfinished revolution, 1863–1877.* Harper Collins.

Gailmard, Sean, and Jeffery Jenkins. 2018. "Distributive politics and congressional voting: Public lands reform in the Jacksonian era." *Public Choice* 175(3): 259–275.

Galor, Oded, and Omer Moav. 2006. "Das Human-Kapital: A theory of the demise of the class structure." *Review of Economic Studies* 73(1): 85–117.

Galor, Oded, Omer Moav, and Dietrich Vollrath. 2009. "Inequality in land-ownership, the emergence of human-capital promoting institutions, and the great divergence." *Review of Economic Studies* 76(1): 143–179.

Garfias, Francisco. 2018. "Elite competition and state capacity development: Theory and evidence from post-revolutionary Mexico." *American Political Science Review* 112(2): 339–357.

Garfias, Francisco. 2019. "Elite coalitions, limited government, and fiscal capacity development: Evidence from Mexico." *Journal of Politics* 81(1): 94–111.

Go, Sun, and Peter Lindert. 2010. "The uneven rise of American public schools to 1850." *Journal of Economic History* 70(01): 1–26.

Goldin, Claudia. 1976. *Urban slavery in the American South, 1820–1860: A quantitative history.* University of Chicago Press.

Goldin, Claudia, and Lawrence F. Katz. 2009. *The race between education and technology*. Harvard University Press.

González, Felipe, Guillermo Marshall, and Suresh Naidu. 2017. "Start-up nation? Slave wealth and entrepreneurship in Civil War Maryland." *Journal of Economic History* 77(2): 373–405.

Goodrich, Carter. 1974. *Government promotion of American canals and railroads, 1800–1890*. Greenwood Press.

Gray, Lewis, and Esther Thompson. 1933. *History of agriculture in the Southern United States to 1860*. Carnegie Institution of Washington.

Green, Fletcher. 1966. *Constitutional development in the South Atlantic states, 1776–1860: A study in the evolution of democracy*. W. W. Norton.

Gregory, James. 2006. *The Southern diaspora: How the great migrations of Black and White Southerners transformed America*. University of North Carolina Press.

Hahn, Steven. 2006. *The roots of Southern populism: Yeoman farmers and the transformation of the Georgia Upcountry, 1850–1890*. Oxford University Press.

Heath, Milton. 1950. "North American railroads: Public railroad construction and the development of private enterprise in the South before 1861." *Journal of Economic History* 10: 40–53.

Hoffman, Philip, and Kathryn Norberg. 1994. *Fiscal crises, liberty, and representative government, 1450–1789*. Stanford University Press.

Hollenbach, Florian. 2021. "Elite interests and public spending: Evidence from Prussian cities." *Review of International Organizations* 16(1): 189–211.

Hyman, Michael. 1989. "Taxation, public policy, and political dissent: Yeoman disaffection in the post-Reconstruction lower South." *Journal of Southern History* 55(1): 49–76.

Jensen, Jeffrey L., Giuliana Pardelli, and Jeffrey Timmons. 2023. "When do elites support increasing taxation? Evidence from the American South." *Journal of Politics* 85(2): 453–467. https://doi.org/10.1086/723806.

Johnson, Michael. 1999. *Toward a patriarchal republic: The secession of Georgia*. Louisiana State University Press.

Keele, Luke, William Cubbison, and Ismail White. 2021. "Suppressing Black votes: A historical case study of voting restrictions in Louisiana." *American Political Science Review* 115(2): 694–700.

Key, V. O. 1984. *Southern politics in state and nation*. University of Tennessee Press.

Keyssar, Alexander. 2001. *The right to vote: The contested history of democracy in the United States*. Basic Books.

Kousser, J. Morgan. 1974. *The shaping of Southern politics: Suffrage restriction and the establishment of the one-party South, 1880–1910*. Vol. 102 Yale University Press.

Larson, John. 2002. *Internal improvement: National public works and the promise of popular government in the early United States*. University of North Carolina Press.

Law, Christopher. 1967. "The growth of urban population in England and Wales, 1801–1911." *Transactions of the Institute of British Geographers* pp. 125–143.

Lee, Alexander, and Jack Paine. 2022. "The great revenue divergence." *International Organization* First View: 1–42.

Leff, Nathaniel. 1997. "Economic development in Brazil, 1822–1913." In *How Latin America fell behind*, ed. Stephen Haber. Stanford University Press, pp. 34–64.

Levi, Margaret. 1988. *Of rule and revenue*. University of California Press.

Lieberman, Evan. 2003. *Race and regionalism in the politics of taxation in Brazil and South Africa*. Cambridge University Press.

Lizzeri, Alessandro, and Nicola Persico. 2004. "Why did the elites extend the suffrage? Democracy and the scope of government, with an application to Britain's 'age of reform.'" *Quarterly Journal of Economics* 119(2): 707–765.

Logan, Trevon. 2019. Whitelashing: Black politicians, taxes, and violence. Technical report National Bureau of Economic Research.

Logan, Trevon. 2020. "Do Black politicians matter? Evidence from Reconstruction." *Journal of Economic History* 80(1): 1–37.

Mares, Isabela, and Didac Queralt. 2015. "The non-democratic origins of income taxation." *Comparative Political Studies* 48(14): 1974–2009.

Mares, Isabela, and Didac Queralt. 2020. "Fiscal innovation in nondemocratic regimes: Elites and the adoption of the Prussian income taxes of the 1890s." *Explorations in Economic History* 77: 101–340.

Margo, Robert. 2007. *Race and Schooling in the South, 1880–1950*. University of Chicago Press.

Marrs, Aaron. 2009. *Railroads in the Old South: Pursuing progress in a slave society*. Johns Hopkins University Press.

Mayshar, Joram, Omer Moav, and Zvika Neeman. 2017. "Geography, transparency, and institutions." *American Political Science Review* 111(3): 622–636.

McCurry, Stephanie. 2012. *Confederate reckoning: Power and politics in the Civil War South*. Harvard University Press.

Meltzer, Allan, and Scott Richard. 1981. "A rational theory of the size of government." *Journal of Political Economy* 89(5): 914–927.

Merritt, Keri Leigh. 2017. *Masterless men: Poor Whites and slavery in the antebellum South.* Cambridge University Press.

Moore, Mick. 2008. "Between coercion and contract: Competing narratives on taxation and governance." In *Taxation and state-building in developing countries*, ed. Deborah Braütigam, Odd-Helge Fjeldstad, and Mick Moore. Cambridge University Press, pp. 34–63.

North, Douglass. 1960. *The economic growth of the U.S., 1790–1860.* Princeton University Press.

North, Douglass, and Barry Weingast. 1989. "Constitutions and commitment: The evolution of institutions governing public choice in seventeenth-century England." *Journal of Economic History* 49(04): 803–832.

Perman, Michael. 2003. *Struggle for mastery: Disfranchisement in the South, 1888–1908.* University of North Carolina Press.

Phillips, Ulrich Bonnell. 1908. *A history of transportation in the eastern Cotton Belt to 1860.* Columbia University Press.

Polanyi, Karl. 1944. *The great transformation.* Beacon Press.

Porter, Kirk. 1918. *A history of suffrage in the United States.* University of Chicago Press.

Queralt, Didac. 2017. "Protection not for sale, but for tax compliance." *International Studies Quarterly* 61(3): 631–641.

Rabushka, Alvin. 2010. *Taxation in colonial America.* Princeton University Press.

Ramsay, David. 1815. *The history of the American Revolution.* Vol. 2. Downing and Phillips.

Ransom, Roger. 2001. "The economics of the Civil War." *EH.net Encyclopedia.*

Ransom, Roger, and Richard Sutch. 2001. *One kind of freedom: The economic consequences of emancipation.* Cambridge University Press.

Reed, Merl. 1962. "Government investment and economic growth: Louisiana's ante-bellum railroads." *Journal of Southern History* 28(2): 183–201.

Reulecke, Jürgen. 1977. "Population growth and urbanization in Germany in the 19th century." *Urbanism Past & Present* (4): 21–32.

Ross, Michael. 2015. "What have we learned about the resource curse?" *Annual Review of Political Science* 18: 239–259.

Saylor, Ryan. 2014. *State building in boom times.* Oxford University Press.

Scheve, Kenneth, and David Stasavage. 2010. "The conscription of wealth: Mass warfare and the demand for progressive taxation." *International Organization* 64(04): 529–561.

Scheve, Kenneth, and David Stasavage. 2016. *Taxing the rich; A history of fiscal fairness in the United States and Europe*. Princeton University Press.

Scheve, Kenneth, and David Stasavage. 2017. "Wealth inequality and democracy." *Annual Review of Political Science* 20: 451–468.

Seligman, Edwin. 1969. *Essays in taxation*. Augustus Kelley.

Sokoloff, Ken, and Eric Zolt. 2006. "Inequality and taxation: Evidence from the Americas on how inequality may influence tax institutions." *Tax Law Review* 59(2): 167–241.

Stasavage, David. 2007. "Partisan politics and public debt: The importance of the 'Whig Supremacy' for Britain's financial revolution." *European Review of Economic History* 11(1): 123–153.

Sun, Liyang, and Sarah Abraham. 2021. "Estimating dynamic treatment effects in event studies with heterogeneous treatment effect." *Journal of Econometrics* 225(2): 175–199.

Suryanarayan, Pavithra, and Steven White. 2021. "Slavery, Reconstruction, and bureaucratic capacity in the American South." *American Political Science Review* 115(2): 568–584.

Sylla, Richard, John Legler, and John Wallis. 1993. *Sources and uses of funds in state and local governments, 1790–1915*. ICPSR.

Thornton, J. Mills. 1982. "Fiscal policy and the failure of radical Reconstruction in the lower South." In *Region, Race, and Reconstruction*, ed. J. Morgan Kousser and James M. McPherson. Oxford University Press, pp. 349–394.

Thornton, J. Mills. 2014. *Politics and power in a slave society: Alabama, 1800–1860*. Louisiana State University Press.

Tilly, Charles. 1975. "Reflections on the history of European state-making." In *The formation of national states in Western Europe*, ed. Charles Tilly. Princeton University Press, pp. 3–83.

Timmons, Jeffrey. 2005. "The fiscal contract: States, taxes, and public services." *World Politics* 57: 530–567.

Timmons, Jeffrey. 2010. "Taxation and credible commitment: Left, right, and partisan turnover." *Comparative Politics* 42(2): 207–227.

Tolnay, Stewart, and Elwood Beck. 1995. *A festival of violence: An analysis of Southern lynchings, 1882–1930*. University of Illinois Press.

Valelly, Richard. 2009. *The two Reconstructions: The struggle for Black enfranchisement*. University of Chicago Press.

Vollrath, Dietrich. 2013. "Inequality and school funding in the rural United States, 1890." *Explorations in Economic History* 50(2): 267–284.

Wallis, John. 2000. "American government finance in the long run: 1790 to 1990." *Journal of Economic Perspectives* 14(1): 61–82.

Wallis, John Joseph. 2005. "Constitutions, corporations, and corruption: American states and constitutional change, 1842 to 1852." *Journal of Economic History* 65(1): 211–256.

Wallis, John, and Barry Weingast. 2018. "Equilibrium federal impotence: Why the states and not the American national government financed economic development in the antebellum era." *Journal of Public Finance and Public Choice* 33(1): 19–44.

Walton, Hanes, Sherman Puckett, and Donald Deskins. 2012. *The African American electorate: A statistical history*. CQ Press.

Wooster, Ralph. 1969. *The people in power: Courthouse and statehouse in the lower South, 1850–1860*. University of Tennessee Press.

Wooster, Ralph. 1975. *Politicians, planters, and plain folk: Courthouse and statehouse in the upper South, 1850–1860*. University of Tennessee Press.

Wright, Gavin. 1978. *The political economy of the cotton South: Households, markets, and wealth in the nineteenth century*. W. W. Norton.

Wright, Gavin. 2022. "Slavery and the rise of the nineteenth-century American economy." *Journal of Economic Perspectives* 36(2): 123–148.

Ziblatt, Daniel. 2009. "Shaping democratic practice and the causes of electoral fraud: The case of nineteenth-century Germany." *American Political Science Review* 103(1): 1–21.

Zolberg, Aristide. 1980. "Strategic interactions and the formation of modern states: france and England." *International Social Science Journal* 32(4): 687–716.

Cambridge Elements ☰

Political Economy

David Stasavage

New York University

David Stasavage is Julius Silver Professor in the Wilf Family Department of Politics at New York University. He previously held positions at the London School of Economics and at Oxford University. His work has spanned a number of different fields and currently focuses on two areas: development of state institutions over the long run and the politics of inequality. He is a member of the American Academy of Arts and Sciences.

About the Series

The Element Series Political Economy provides authoritative contributions on important topics in the rapidly growing field of political economy. Elements are designed so as to provide broad and in depth coverage combined with original insights from scholars in political science, economics, and economic history. Contributions are welcome on any topic within this field.

Cambridge Elements $\equiv$

Political Economy

Elements in the Series

A full series listing is available at: www.cambridge.org/EPEC

Printed in the United States
by Baker & Taylor Publisher Services